AGONIES *and* ECSTASIES

AGONIES *and* ECSTASIES

ALEXANDER RILEY

RESOURCE *Publications* · Eugene, Oregon

AGONIES AND ECSTASIES

Resource Publications
An Imprint of Wipf and Stock Publishers
199 W. 8th Ave., Suite 3
Eugene, OR 97401

www.wipfandstock.com

PAPERBACK ISBN: 979-8-3852-6207-6
HARDCOVER ISBN: 979-8-3852-6208-3
EBOOK ISBN: 979-8-3852-6209-0

11/17/25

CONTENTS

PREFACE: AGONIES
AND ECSTASIES

IT IS REMARKABLE that we find so much of life so unremarkable. Our capacity for autopilot, for experiencing large chunks of our time walking the earth in a state of impassive calm or boredom, fits poorly with the objectively startling fact of being alive in a universe overwhelmingly dominated by the inert.

It is nonetheless how all of us experience almost all of the time we are conscious. Doing something while not even really aware that you are doing it is the story of the great majority of our hours and days. It is as if the body is performing the actions required by the activity without any need for input from the mind, or at least any activity of the mind taking place in these moments is as mundane and formulaic as the action it accompanies. In this vast percentage of our waking time, we are as somnambulists, externally moving about but internally thoroughly unmoved.

Then there are the rare moments and experiences that take you out of that mundanity and thrust you into some other place. In this place, everything is different. Here, you are alive, fully alive. Not merely breathing and conscious but filled with an emotional energy scarcely touchable by description. The experience is so intense that it encompasses evident contradictions. Elated but melancholic, redeemed yet doomed, potent to the nth degree but more deeply aware than at any other moment of the fragile and delicate state of everything and of its unbearable yet exhilarating finitude, exploding with love for the entirety of creation but haughtily superior in the way of gods looking down on a fallen world.

This experience is of totality. All of every capacity the mind holds is maximized here. In such moments, one is taken outside the limits of the finiteness of the everyday. The extremity of these experiences might be described as either ecstatic or as agonizing, or, more commonly, as some pulsating and complex combination of both of these seeming contraries. The most central element of the experience is the feeling of being intoxicated with the hypnotic certainty that there exists nothing beyond what is present just then, and the triumph of the illusion that one will never, ever die.

I have tried, with limited hope concerning the possibility of success, to write some of those moments, to capture them in the bottle of magic that is writing, and to communicate them to others in a form that might evoke something of the experience itself. The effort is certain to be a failed one in advance. Only the experience is the experience. No words about it are sufficient to make it manifest for the reader. I fully understand and accept it. I make no other excuse than that the residue of those experiences compelled me to an effort that was doomed in advance. As when in the grip of the sacred, I had no choice but to go along for the ride, and I wanted nothing else.

WAKE

WITH THE ANNOYING BUZZ OF an alarm, and often these days driven frantically by a straining bladder demanding to be drained, I swim achingly up out of the bottomless sea of nightly unconsciousness, the light appearing first as a dim shimmering, then a fuzzy glow, finally the illuminated crispness of reality.

For an instant, uncertainty as to whether I will be able to break through the barrier, and then it is sundered. I surge upward, exploding from the depths.

What is this unexpected grace? How can it be? Alive? Again?!

In Mexico, when a friend beholds you coming down the street, he invariably greets you with "*!Qué milagro!*"—*What a miracle!*—even if he just saw you a few days earlier. The meaning is literal, so far as I can tell by the animation of speakers who have uttered those words to me. What an utter and astounding surprise to find you still here! Thank God, you are not dead yet! The purest, unalloyed joy just to see the friend's face, still animated and uninhabited by worms, above ground, breathing, emoting, living.

They have discovered a profound truth. This should be our feeling every morning. Rarely, I achieve it, inexplicably bursting through the crust of habituation and the general human drag away from astonishment and marvel, through no effort or credit of my own. On blessed days, mornings kissed by the holy, it just descends upon me, this joyous awareness that I have not perished in the unsoundable depths of the night. What an overwhelming relief to still be alive! To have successfully navigated another journey through Lethe, through the stillness that is to all appearances indistinguishable from death save for the slight rise and fall of the chest and the intake and exhalation of air that is its cause. The rushing back in of consciousness is for all that nearly identical, according to my perceptual palate at least, to an actual return from the dead.

Try, just try to imagine all the things that could have gone wrong in the night as you slept but did not. All the many, so many things that could have gone awry and caused your demise.

Your heart could have just stopped, for no easily explicable reason whatsoever. This happens with a frequency one does well to avoid thinking about too much. Every thirty seconds or so, someone in America dies of heart disease. Three hundred fifty thousand perish every year because their hearts abruptly cease to function, without advance warning, seemingly without cause, at least until autopsy. It is uncommon for young, healthy people to turn in on a given night and then just fail to wake, but this is little comfort for those of us for whom youth is gone and for whom the dreadful probability rises every year, every month, every week, every night.

The disappearance into the sleep of death has been a terror for us since the day we became aware that a finitude, a final, unappealable end comes for each of us, and therefore for the one thinking the thought too. The night, the blackness, the quiet, the absence, all thick with foreboding and secrets and the most basic and unmitigated of our fears. Songs and tales by the fire before the coming of the nightly tempting of destiny were our means to warm our souls as our bodies against the chill of the void.

Mysterious, terrifying, perhaps death in the night is to do with some structural defect unimagined, something you never knew about and indeed never would have learned about unless it killed you, in which case you still never learn about it because it did bring your end, and others are left to be introduced to the occluded and fatal fact, and then to dread its possible presence in their own bodies, lurking, waiting for the propitious time to strike. Inexplicable, a failure in the electric system of the cardiovascular system. Random lethality. No sense whatever. Here, asleep, pleasantly and warmly wrapped in blankets and dreams, and then abruptly gone, forever, eternally.

Death can come otherwise. The house could catch fire and violently shatter your blissful peace to face the nightmare of a trapped and tortured conclusion to your life's drama, your lungs filling and suffocating on smoke as black as the night engulfing it, your skin blistering and then melting in the seconds of shattering pain that seem as eternities before the blissful nothing finally returns to retrieve you from your brief interlude among the conscious.

The tree in the front yard could blow over in a storm and land at precisely the right angle on the roof of your house to come crashing against your head and strike you instantly into permanent quietus in your slumber so quickly as to not even allow your ears to capture the sound of the collapse of the structure of the edifice you believed would shelter you from such events.

You could accidentally leave the car running in the attached garage, with the door open, allowing the carbon monoxide from the exhaust to penetrate into the house and block your red blood cells from absorbing and transporting oxygen, and thus your brain will be arrested in its activity, perhaps right in the middle of a tantalizingly beautiful nocturnal vision, your last, about wafting gently upward on a carpet of glowing cloud toward a distant mountain range.

It is morbid to reflect on these things, I am informed by one who loves me dearly. I cannot criticize her instincts. But she has missed the elation behind my attention to such thoughts.

For if I wake up, then the awful thing did not happen, and in enumerating some of the ways it could have taken place but did not, I am not dwelling on the horrible entity. I am expressing my otherwise incommunicable gratitude to have somehow, by the grace of an enigmatical but beneficent God avoided these various ends. I am sending a thankful prayer to probability for having fallen on my side. For having won the dice roll.

This time. Another time, perhaps I will not be so lucky. At some point, inevitably so. Inexorably, unavoidably, with dreadful certainty, my time will run out.

But today, as the photons of the sun's light burn into my eyes, I am, just this one more time, awake.

I live!

SPIRITS OF DEAD ROCK STARS

CRISP EARLY EVENING IN LATE WINTER, the snow and ice finally melted away, but the air still bitingly brisk. I leave the heat of the house clad in track pants, two shirts and a jacket, and heavy work gloves. I am headed to the school playground nearby, where a jungle gym awaits.

I begin.

I hang from a bar, arms fully extended, then slowly and exactingly pull myself up, taking care to mind my newly healed wrist, ready for the twinge or the ache.

I dip down from other bars, descending as low as possible, then push back up to lock my elbows.

I put my feet up on a bench and lower my chest to the ground, then thrust my torso off the ground, straighten arms, then bend them again to kiss the dirt. The smell of the grass and soil, still damp with recently melted snow, fills my nostrils.

Between sets, I run sprints up a small hill nearby, then return to the bars and the bench.

The fire of pain welcomes me to the threshold. That, and the vague anxiety that this time that traditional payment will not be accepted, is the tariff that must be paid to make it across, into that other space.

No way except through it, straight through. And thus has it always been.

This is a form of torture, an affliction sought, pursued, a scourging that could easily be avoided but that I purposefully bring on myself through this deliberate action.

Here is what it is not, what it cannot be, what I must assiduously work to prevent myself from ever imagining it could be. It is not some vain project in self-cultivation, in the effort to preserve health and to push back aging, decrepitude, and death, though it will contribute to those ends. These are not the reasons I chase this pain.

This is a very exact and exacting form of self-mortification. It is the agony of the piacular rite, the self-inflicted suffering that witnesses one's madness at the loss of the clan member taken away from the ranks by death.

That is the pain I want, the pain I need, the pain that is my one true love, the companion of my deepest desire, as it floods through my body. It is at once a testament to one's brotherly affection for the lost one, torn from us by fate, and the payment exacted for his entry into the realm of the dead.

But what dead?

The dead whose voices I hear shrieking to me from somewhere beyond this place. The plastic devices planted firmly in my ears are now the window into the world of souls.

For our fathers, there was no possibility of hearing the dead after death, short of visitation from beyond. Now, thanks to the accomplishments of our modern wizards, we can daily experience the verbal presence of those who are physically removed from our world.

In my ears proliferate the primal growls and screams of men who died young, still bursting with life. All of their heat, their anger, their fear, their angst, their lust and their love, all of it is here, in my ears, inside my head through the magic of the physics of bodily membranes set vibrating by waves in a gas, which then are transferred along to bones inside the head and a fluid-filled structure and microscopic hair-like projections that open up pores in which chemicals produce electric charges that then travel along the auditory nerve and incite neurons in the brain to turn these waves become chemicals become electricity into the indescribable feeling that I will never die.

I do this work for them, these deceased men, these souls disembodied and now left to roam ghostly through the ears and cochleae and neurons of those like me who yet live, who for a moment more can push past the pain of exertion to someplace higher.

Every word I said is what I mean . . .

I am smellin' like the rose that somebody gave me on my birthday deathbed . . .

What would you do if I followed you? . . .

No one to cry to, no place to call home . . .

See my heart, I decorate it like a grave . . .

Out in the sunshine, the sun is mine . . .

Thus do the voices of men my own age, born in the same year I was born or a year before or a year after, so close to the time that I too began my sojourn on this globe, human companions who were born with me and who are no longer here, thus do their voices echo in my haunted brain yet another time, in the interim, in anticipation of the time when I too will be gone to that place that has become their home.

Night has silently fallen during my ordeal. The sky above is now the black of frozen, timeless space, the nothing that engulfs us, punctuated with little scintillating dots of diamond dust, sparkling, brilliant, penetrating though the size only of grains of sand, indicating innumerable distant worlds larger by far than the one on which I stand, galaxies of expanse so vast that they cannot even be imagined in the same thought as something as inconsequential as the rock on which I stand.

A pregnant moon glows warmly, tempering the chill night air, embracing me in the hope that what I am doing allows my dead brothers to live again, in some vicarious, illogical, spiritually insane, delirious, and weeping manner that eludes all the true things.

The merely true things, those that we praise overmuch and that should now, as we look up at that void, appear as nothing, those things that are ultimately of no use. All that emptiness in the firmament of heaven is my home, and I am here, and they too.

For no one has left. That is the magic I accomplish with the torture I inflict on my body.

No one has left.

All these dead, whose voices ring in my ears, are still here, right here, with me as I grip the bars and pull myself up, up, away from the earth, and toward that swirling sea of opacity.

THE IMPOSSIBLE

THE BELIEF IS STRONG, and thus the disappointment is still more devastating when it comes, as inevitably come it does.

The words will be true, one tells oneself, hopes, prays. The bond will be made. The two minds will meet. The souls will share in a moment of sacred exchange and mutual aid, in perfect unity and completion and the overjoyed solution of the puzzle of isolation and aloneness.

Is this not how it is always described in the literature on friendship and conversation and the sharing of spiritual conviviality and the deepest truths? Transparency. Authenticity. The opening of two human persons to one another, mutually.

For as long as we have had language, in all likelihood, we have been telling ourselves this story, confident in its unarguable truth. Certain that such a thing is not only feasible but that a full human life is not possible without it.

Words are alleged to produce meaning in a basically objective way, even if there is acknowledgement of some role for context. We would not teach our children to speak and to read and to write as we do if we did not believe that when someone utters a word to another this second understands it in the same way as the utterer, and this neat linguistic mathematics is what makes it possible for communication to work. We speak with the child, and we use a word she does not know. We refer to other words she does know to infer the meaning of the new word, or we point to something in the world, or we mime some action. In every case, we trust that the child fills all that up with just the symbols and thoughts and emotions that we have when we speak the new word.

Our faith in this process is unquestioned.

～

Yet there is no reason to believe it to be true. None whatsoever.

Take the word "car." What precisely does that word indicate? *What does it mean?*

A car is a large metallic object on wheels with a motor that propels it and seats that allow humans to ride along.

OK.

But *for me*, that word contains other information inextricably and convolutedly tied to my own experiences and personality.

When I hear "car," there in my mind appears the blown head gasket on the white '76 Chevy Nova that I repaired with a library-borrowed Chilton manual in my college years. I see the worn object now, with the vivid signs of deterioration and the crack that caused the car's exhaust to cloud up and that would eventually have incapacitated the machine. And I feel again the glorious sense of virile affirmation I felt after I had completed the repair when the mechanic father of a childhood friend expressed his minimalist but unmistakable approval of the quality of my work.

There is the fact that this same car—which is for me the *ur-car*, the original, the prototype of the term that always flits at least briefly into my head when I think of the word—had no reverse gear, and so it had to be pushed out of some parking spaces. And that I spray painted it gaudy neon colors with cryptic messages that earned me frequent unwanted attention from law enforcement.

There is the Thanksgiving I spent sitting shivering in the front seat of another car, an Opel station wagon, after sleeping there the night before, my blood congealing in sub-zero temperatures, half-buried under snow the plows had cleared from the highway somewhere in Indiana. This car had broken down there in the middle of the night on the way home for the holiday, in a time before cell phones, and on a day and in weather in which already reduced traffic was still more intermittent, which meant I had to wait despairingly long hours for someone to stop and take me to a nearby town for a tow truck, and I missed the entire holiday dinner.

There is my 2nd grade obsession with Racer X and his car, the Shooting Star, and the car of his brother Speed Racer, the Mach V. The sprint home from school every day to watch the program, and the worshipful drawings I made of those mythological vehicles in my school notebooks. The way they populated my boyish mind in every waking hour and in many of my dreams.

There is my vivid memory of driving off a freeway ramp into traffic on another snowy road and losing control of the vehicle utterly and sitting helpless in the driver's seat as the car spun around several times at 60 mph and skidded across four lanes of busy traffic. And believing with my entire consciousness in these instants that I was milliseconds away from being dead, before somehow flying unharmed into a ditch on the other side of the roadway and sitting there stunned and silent and not at all sure how the miracle that jerked me out of the jaws of destruction had happened, or even that it had happened and that I was not already a shade, for a full half hour before my heart rate slowed and I regained enough composure to get out and seek help in dragging the car back on to the road.

There is the invigorating, sometimes terrifying race I ran most days during a year of grad school in a broken-down, rusted out Pinto at the extreme end of its lifespan, revving up to full speed (perhaps 45 mph, on a good day) coming down the Escondido Freeway toward Kensington, beseeching God to allow me to get up enough momentum to make it up the hill before the rush hour San Diego traffic at my rear ran right over me.

There are the several times I drove cross country from Ohio or Pennsylvania to Oregon or California, across the Midwestern flatlands and the Rockies and the Sonoran, Chihuahuan, and Mojave deserts, and stopped at the Great Salt Lake for a sacramental lunch of crackers and warm soda and discovered viscerally the cold of the American Southwest after sunset by sleeping roadside in the back seat in deep southern Arizona and unintentionally but unavoidably flattened innumerable jackrabbits in the middle of the night roaring out of Winnemucca, losing my transmission in Colorado and my exhaust pipe in Indiana and the U-Haul trailer that was attached to my rear bumper, along with the rear bumper itself, in Missouri, having my cassette tape collection stolen while swimming at a roadside lake in Iowa, and watching the temperature gauge stay steadily and menacingly buried deep in the red in a stretch of the Texas panhandle in August when I was certain the car would explode at any moment and somehow it kept going until I got to some water, and my cat hiding from me in a dingy motel somewhere in New Mexico and forcing me to dismantle the bed to get her out, and that magical day driving across Wyoming under a perfect fall sky listening to three Tangerine Dream tapes over and over, and once going 2700 miles in just over two days, sleeping in the driver's seat for two fitful five hour stretches while feverish with a mystery viral infection, empty cans of Red Bull all over the floorboards, and descending down from the mountains east of San Diego on the I-8 as some kind of modern-day Greek deity emerging majestically from the clouds, with Mexican cumbia music blasting from my ruptured speakers, feeling as though it was the very choir of Heaven serenading me home at the conclusion of a mechanized odyssey.

There is the feel of every steering wheel I have ever held, the tension of every gas pedal I have depressed, the squeak of brakes too long neglected, the smell of upholstery and floor carpeting soaked with rain and snow and grease and spilled coffee and the drippings from many species of fast food.

There is my visceral refusal to participate in or even to attempt to understand the romance of my society with the car as status symbol, the widespread desire to purchase and then drive the kind of car that tells the watching world—and, more importantly, tells the driver—that he occupies an enviable position in a hierarchy, and there is also the strange and irreconcilable validation I felt when, in my mid-thirties, I finally commanded enough wealth to purchase a car that had not been previously owned by someone else, the overwhelming relief that I had now joined something called "the middle class" and could perhaps let up a little bit.

There is the vomit on the back seat of the white Nova in which I lay after drinking too much Schnapps, with a stomach full of oatmeal cream pies, and the odor that never quite came out despite all the scrubbing and that became as inescapable a feature of that car as the fact that it had four wheels, a smell I always immediately associated with my mortality, since it had been the merest of accidents that in my inebriated stupor I had regurgitated the contents of my stomach before falling asleep and not after, and if it had happened after I lost consciousness I might never have regained it.

The word "car" contains all that for me, all that and more, far more than I can say, much that sits somewhere below my awareness and yet profoundly informs my reaction when I hear that word. Others have their own memories, incompatible with mine.

All this slippage, all this lost context and inexplicable detail of experience, it is true, it does not prevent us accomplishing mundane business with the word "car."

But we do not mean the same thing when we use it.

And if we cannot even mean the same thing, if we cannot even get on the same communicative page when we want to talk of a lump of metal and plastic and rubber, what fantasy could lead us to believe we do when what we desire to discuss is Art, or the Good, or Love, or God?

~

And so, the failure of the conversation of even the closest of friends is inevitable. How could it be otherwise? It is destined to fail from the start by the nature of the tools we bring to the task.

Yet, that promise that repeats itself every time at the cusp, just before, just before the truth intrudes, mercilessly, inevitably, yet again . . .

That promise is so profoundly spiritually energizing, it fills me with such joy and anticipation and ecstasy to be alive and to be on the brink of something that will change my life. It is so pure and so good that even its eternal failure to materialize is not sufficient to reduce its essential place in a universe such as the one we inhabit.

I will take it, happily, all in my awareness of its eternal inability to make good on its celestial promise.

TONY AND TIFFANY

THE LAST DAY OF EIGHTH grade, prelude to what would be the summer before my first year of high school. The world suddenly growing much larger than it had been previously. What would it bring, this pulsating, vibrant moment of chrysalis?

In the last few weeks before vacation, there was a budding romance, my first, a tall girl with blonde hair cut in a bob and blue eyes and an endearingly askew smile.

Her name was Tiffany.

She was the first girl whose hand I had held who was not my sister. First time of that indescribable experience, anticipation, marvel, longing, exhilaration. The very first time. Full of a longing that had made a familiar world entirely new and strange, I saw her every day, in the next to last class of the day, and I saw her on that last day of school before the blissful release into the late spring sun. Her family name evoked the joyous melody that played in my head whenever her face came before my gaze.

I could not believe the gods had so smiled on me. It was as though this had been planned somewhere. If I had been offered any other life at that moment in exchange for this one I had in which I got to hold the hand of this precious girl and call her by her name, I would have refused it.

On that day, in the last class of the last day, I spoke with a friend. He was a boy I knew well. Our mothers worked together, he had slept at my house, I at his, and we had held those conversations in the dark just before sleep that young people have, about dreams and nightmares and hopes and fears. We had eaten meals together, this boy and I. He was thin like me, though not very tall, with longish straight brown hair, a sweet almost feminine disposition, friendly with everyone, a laugh that was easy and full. He was headed after school to the hair salon where our two mothers worked, while I was going home. I told him I would see him later.

His name was Tony.

We were all so full of excitement and energy that day. Twenty 14- and 15-year-olds, chomping at life's bit, on the cusp of summer break, ready to get everything underway with abandon as the bell rang and out we streamed into our lives and into the world.

When I got home—after a leisurely, beatific half hour walk, talking with a friend about a new album, stopping at the store for a can of soda, planning the next day's baseball or basketball, filled with the delicious pleasure not only of what was happening right then but of what was to come in the next several months of bike riding and swimming and sitting on the porch in conversation and playing guitar and mostly of spending time with the tall blonde girl with the heartbreakingly adorable smile—the phone rang. It was my mother, calling from work.

I could tell she was crying.

Tony, my friend, her friend's first born, the boy I had just seen in that room only a half hour earlier with all of our rowdy cohort of teens, to whom I had with cheer and conviction said "See ya later!" as we separated at the end of the school day, Tony, my friend Tony, *Tony was dead.*

There had been an accident. He was on his bike, on a busy avenue, a street that bore the name for beneficed members of the clergy, and therefore symbolically in communion with God, though populated by whiskey joints and broken people. On this holy and unholy road, there had been a tractor trailer turning a corner, and the driver had not seen my friend on his bike, who was unaware the metal behemoth at his side was preparing to swerve right into his path. It took but a few seconds for this to occur.

A few seconds.

Just before, he had stopped by the shop where his mother and mine were working, and he had spoken with the woman who brought him into this world, who could not know then that she was hearing her son's voice for the last time, for the last time in his life and hers and in the life of everyone else on this planet, the last time he would speak any words at all forever. He had stopped to speak with his mother. As though he knew.

Tony was dead.

The boy I had only just seen with my own two eyes, just heard speak with my own two ears, just touched as our hands clasped in a brotherly farewell, confident we would see one another again in short order.

I could not weep because I could not believe it to be true. Confused, I wondered why my mother would tell me such a thing, as I was certain that it could not be so.

A few days later, at the funeral home, all of us from school gathered. Everyone knew him. The casket was closed, so we could not even see his face one last time. He was just gone. Only a box in his place there before the crowd.

Those words we exchanged on the last day of school before I falsely told him that I would see him again soon. What were they? I tried to recall what I had said to him, the one who was at that instant that I spoke, all without our knowing, standing at the threshold of the next world. What did he say, the departing one, what words did he speak to me, what might Destiny have put on his lips to give to me as life advice? An occluded warning? A prediction?

I could not recall any of the words, try as I would. I would give much now to be able to retrieve them. I have tried to convince myself many times over the years that I had suddenly remembered what he said, but every time, after a moment's reflection, I knew it was invention, my mind creating something to give my heart some peace over something that I should have remembered but that now is gone forever, as is my friend.

As I stood there in the room where his corpse lay hidden, I could plainly see his face, which I would never see again, as though it were there in front of mine. I see it still now, more than four decades later.

The tall blonde girl was there, her face wet with tears.

I still had not cried, and I was so distraught it did not even occur to me how incongruous I must have seemed in that room of weeping teenagers. It was not real.

She came to me, and, wordlessly, I held her while she sobbed.

It was here, in this place, in this setting, with this on my heart and in my soul, this was the first time I had held a girl in my arms. I felt her warm body beside mine, her budding breasts beneath her shirt, and her tears fell on my neck as she cried, burning with the heat of love and the vigor of youthful life and the anguish before the inexplicable death of a child who should have had sixty more years before him. I wanted to cry, desperately now, but still no tears came.

It was overwhelming to be here, he in that box at the front of the room, and she in my arms at the back of it. Incongruous, yet somehow delicately balanced and very exactly and precisely accurate, a scale of the world set at perfect equilibrium between life and its negation.

I was fourteen years old, just. Was this the world, then? This? Love and death, all mixed up together and inextricable. Was this the world?

WALTZ

JUST OUT OF COLLEGE, I lived in a rented room on the second floor of a home that sat in a little town in the mountains of a Western state almost three thousand miles from where I grew up.

A nice elderly lady owned the place. She did not ask me anything when I came to inquire about it, and she was not put off by my long hair or the fact that my car had spray-painted graffiti and arcane sketches in fluorescent orange, green, and yellow across its length and breadth. I imagined she had seen a few like me in her time, out here in the West, and knew we were a mostly harmless subspecies. We might fail to keep jobs and drive too fast, but despite what we sometimes said we were not really going to burn down your culture, as that was too much work, and we were mostly just interested in finding a reliable bass player for the band.

The stairway up to my room was narrow and carpeted. Dirty in the unavoidable way that carpeted stairs are, worn-in grime from the bottoms of shoes that could have come all the way from the other side of the country, as my shoes and I had. We had traveled there, those thousands of miles, out I-70, across the plains, up and through the Rockies, and down across the endless desert, in a car for which I had paid a hundred dollars cash, an old Chevy with more than a hundred fifty thousand miles on it and a transmission with no reverse and a bashed-in, duct-taped rear windshield and a rusted hole in the driver-side floorboard through which you could see the road below you as it went by at 60 mph.

The house stank of cigarettes, as there were other boarders who smoked heavily, though I never saw any of them, not even once. My room was the second one on the left after mounting the stairs. The room just after mine was the bathroom, and there were two more rooms on the opposite side, four in total. Tiny, cramped, a rickety bed and an aged nightstand and a chair with peeling upholstery, and dully flowered wallpaper that purveyed an unintended mournfulness. I had no television or radio, and I desired neither. Sometimes I could hear ambient television sound in the evenings from the rooms around me, but never enough to discern anything sensible. It was not even clear that the noise I heard emanating from the walls was human in origin. I slept atop the covers and used a coat as a blanket, like a railway hobo. The elderly lady asked me from time to time about washing the bedding, but I told her it was fine.

In this room, I sat sullen for hours, days, weeks, months, an entire winter, hiding from the person I had been just a short while before.

I would leave the room only to go to work at the bookstore where I impatiently manned the cash register and aristocratically, imperiously judged everyone who purchased a Danielle Steele or Louis L'Amour novel, which was nearly everyone who entered the store. Tried to push Tolstoy and Flaubert from the used books bin to no avail. *The Bookworm*, the place was called, and in my youthful and misplaced confidence in my own intellectual elevation I never tired of mocking the lack of fit between this name and the clientele. The owner was an odd, affable guy named George who had retired from some other line of work with substantial money, got into used books because he liked the Rabbit novels of John Updike, which he endlessly recommended to me. I never read them and mildly resented him for presuming to tell the future great writer I planned to be what good literature was.

From work, I would drive to the open market and steal vegetables and fruit, eating them surreptitiously right there standing before the racks, quickly and discreetly. There were no cameras in such places in those days. Then back to the room to read, write in my journal, listen to music, grapple with the what and the why of a life that was hurtling menacingly but seductively toward me.

The cigarette smoke wafted in from the room next door. The guy who lived there had a daily coughing fit in the morning, lasting perhaps fifteen minutes, furious, violent hacking. Then, when it ended, the cigarette smoke came. Once he had cleared his throat, it was time to foul it back up. Did he know death was stalking him, as Don Juan says in the Castaneda book that all rebels read or say they have read and that I was lazily perusing at the time? (I never finished it). It was stalking me too, though my youth mostly kept me from fully reckoning with that.

I did get this point sufficiently to sit bleary-eyed, in the middle of the night, listening to works by a composer introduced to me by a friend, who had made enough of a career as an artist to merit the title "painter." A few images of his work can now even be found online, and his papers are held in a university archive. I thought what he did was remarkable, a marvelous incandescent symbolism. He sent me some postcard prints of a few works once, and I have misplaced them in my piles and piles of memories. I hope one day, miraculously, to fall upon them again, as I am sure such a discovery would bring me delirious joy.

He was a man close to seventy, from Chicago, some kind of Eastern European ancestry, jovial, worldly, wise. He completely changed my mind about some things, though I knew him only a few months. Later, when I moved away, he wrote me a handful of letters, colorful details of artistic life in the language and the script of a real character. I did not respond to him often enough. He died decades ago, and I did not know he was gone until much later. This is how we drift away from one another and then it is too late. I wish I could hear his voice again, but it cannot be.

My friend, this painter spoke to me, saying "You will adore this, listen, listen!" with twinkling eyes, and he was right, as happens with experienced older people. It was an American composer of the twentieth century, still alive at the time, the first American composer I had heard that I liked, in my youthful disdain for everything cultural to do with my own country. This composer, the Fates had decreed, was born near the very place I inhabited when I discovered his work.

In the wee hours in that smoke-fouled house, in the humble little room that contained all my meager belongings, I prayerfully explored several cassettes of this music, dubbed and gifted by my friend. There was an exotic-sounding string quartet set, developmentally melancholy, studied sadness, slow and funereal, ranging from reflection on medieval song to four-part Baroque counterpoint. And there was a bit from a symphony, an interlude, after a grandiose opening few movements of vast proportions, a delicate, weeping melody on strings, a little more than two minutes that I repeated reverentially, endlessly until I was too tired to go on, until I collapsed and the melody lurked in my sleeping mind in the way I told myself—because Baudelaire or Poe had written it—a dead lover must.

That melody so lachrymose, so otherworldly, that it filled my eyes with tears and my soul with love for all things on hearing the first strains, poured into my soul an ocean of compassion for all the beings that ever dwelt on this stone orbiting the distant star, all those who lived and died and then disappeared unceremoniously into the ether. Compassion too for myself, who was hurtling toward that same horizon but at the time, since I saw that end as something yet to arrive, postponed, distant, at the time sufficiently composed to experience that self-feeling as contentment.

My life then was becoming something I did not recognize, something already fully beyond all my efforts to exert any control over it. I had once had a plan, but it had changed, and I did not know anything more than that. College was done, and it was not clear what would come next except trepidation. My family were all far away, in miles and in spirit. I had abandoned most of my friends and just recently broken with the only one besides the painter who lived within a day's drive, telling him to forget he knew me. I knew not why I had done all of this. It was as though I watched someone else acting in my body. Looking on at some force at work I could not fathom. I was fearful of what was still to come for me, yet expectant.

Weeping for myself and for all of us, I sat on that bed, listening, thankful without knowing it that the woman for whom the piece was named had lived so the composer would have the inspiration to produce this little piece of magic that spoke so eloquently and movingly to me of the impossibility of escape from myself.

OVERHEAD, THE MOON

FULL, RADIANT BEACON, ILLUMINATING the clouds that pass by so swiftly that their motion gives one the only impression one can have from a point on this world that the whole of the thing on which we pass our lives is hurtling through space at speeds that defy every bit of sensory data generated by our poor animal mechanism.

Looking up, at that permanence that is still not quite permanent, but closer certainly than any of the paltry concerns with which we pass our days and which keep us awake at night, gazing with neck tilted, eyes to the heavens, at this celestial body a fourth the size of Earth passing only a few hundred thousand miles away, not even a hundred times greater than the distance I have driven in a matter of a few days with little rest, I feel certain that nothing goes through my mind that did not also occur to my forebears of 50,000 years ago as they looked skyward and had their gaze magnetically fixed, as is mine, without any exertion of will, automatically and inevitably, to this ghostly visitor in the night.

How vast, the span of the black sky that looms over my head, over and behind and beyond the tops of the trees that dwarf me, the canvas on which that globe is graven and hung. In every direction from here into that void spin unseen stars and unperceived planets, innumerable, a quantity my mind could not fathom, even to see it represented in the symbols my primate fellows invented.

How small am I, standing below these trees, watching this vast tableau above, how irrelevant to what occurs, as I stand watching, on all those countless worlds, all the dust storms and the volcanic explosions and the freezing gusts of wind and the lonely motion of the stray particles of unknown elements finding their determined destination after a voyage planned billions of years ago in the celestial mind of the universe.

Worlds are born and die as I gaze upward, unaware, unknowing.

How perfect this world into which I have been thrown. Perfect in its beauty, perfect in its hope, perfect too in its darkness, and its cruelty, and its despair, and its refusal ever to yield to our desires, especially to our desire to know it and thereby tame it and make it our own.

When I was a boy, I would think of mysteries like that of this unfathomable night sky, and I would be frightened, until I remembered that those adults who cared for me—my mother, my father, my grandparents, all the others who loved me and would look out for me in their wisdom and solicitude—were possessed of insights I did not have, of power I could not imagine, of authority and efficacy of which I could scarcely dream. Then I would be calmed, at the mere thought of those who I knew must know things I did not.

I think of my children, in their turn trusting in their confidence that I, their father, have figured out essential things, when the truth is that I know nothing, am nothing, and all of us are careening off into the heart of a void so vast that it defies our every effort to articulate any relationship to it at all.

The absurd and total quietude of life, the pristine silence of all of humanity, alone in the shadow, save for that spectral globe hung, painted, carved there, out of the black unending canvas on which it sits, a canvas that was never made and will never be unmade, that has been hung there by a force we do not dare comprehend at the beginning of time that had no beginning, that extends everywhere, forever, world without end.

All my kin asleep, or so it seems, though Australia bustles unknown underneath me as I stand in the dark.

How good, how indisputably good the design of a world that occludes that knowledge from my sensory machinery, making me the sole observer of our fate, as I contemplate the message the moon brings to me about my own place in the vast emptiness on which it reflects the rays of an unseen sun.

KEYBOARD AESTHETICS

A PIANIST AT THE KEYS. A human body set before a device with 88 little levers, hands curved and fingers poised to press them and thereby extract from them the delightful essence we call music.

The unspeakable beauty of the form.

The jazz virtuoso, the impossible fluency and physical presence. As though the thing is not an object external at all, but an extension of the hands. The marvel of that deceptive perception. The way of the hand, the right side of the equation yielded by the addition of years of repetition of the same scalar pathways until they are carved into the very body and the unfathomable source of inspiration.

When a lovely young woman, jet black hair and eyes, ruby lips, voluptuous geometry of her entire being, silky bare arms, with certainty and precision interprets the creative life of a long dead genius, her pulchritude and the passionate expertise of her skill combine to steal away my breath. Both originate in the same source, and each merits the same rapt awe and yearning. She, all of her, is a gift.

A magician, conjuring Bach. So slow, so measured, he seems drifting in a light breeze, his hands waving and rising and descending in majestic arcs, settling on the keys at the perfect moment to produce the needed tone, a shaman conjuring ghosts or visions of the future. This is what it must have been like to see, a hundred thousand years ago, a mystic hallucinogenically speaking to beings from the dream world, magical and authentic. He is Art defined.

That hat, the stiff body which yet communicates the essence of the human itself when he stands and walks around jerkily, absently, joyously dancing while the rest of the band plays. The peculiar idiosyncrasy of poking and jabbing at notes that somehow do not sound poked and jabbed but are instead like liquifying butter on warm toast and a cup of hot coffee with sugar and cream. He seems to have no idea what he is doing, and this is the essence of his craft.

An Englishman, with a spangled vest, and many keyboards, standing the organ on its end, spinning it around, slamming it to the floor, stabbing it with knives, mingling the beauty of Mussorgsky and the power of rock 'n' roll, fully awakening the fire of music in the heart of the boy watching, and oh so carefully and reverently, listening. Listening.

THE SCARY MOVIE

I AM WATCHING IT ON MY PHONE, with headphones on, at 1:06 am, while everyone else is in the other half of the house, deep in slumber.

In the film, they look for someone in a deserted house, and then there is a shout from off camera. It is recorded in such a way that it sounds somehow like it came from the other room of my own house.

Initially, I suspect someone has called to me from one of the bedrooms. Perhaps my wife, reminding me of something happening in the morning. Our youngest, requesting a drink of water. I pause the film, take out the earpiece, listen. Nothing.

I scroll the film back fifteen seconds. The sound from the other room again. Again, I am fooled and pause the film a second time to listen to what must be emanating from the other half of my house, which is shrouded in darkness.

Then, in the second, the micro-second, before my brain makes the logical connection and I realize the sound came from the film, the trepidation the film had produced in the part of me that is following that cinematic narrative instantly travels to neurons in the part of my brain that is not engaged with the film, and I have a sudden, intense pang of mortal fear that an intruder is somewhere in the house, preparing to spring lethally upon me or upon my sleeping loved ones in the bedrooms. It is the progress of that malevolent being toward his dreadful goal that I am hearing, and I have discerned it too late to prevent its terrible achievement.

It is an exquisite terror.

It only lasts the blink of an eye and then reason unceremoniously and brutally removes it. It cannot be so. There is no unseen killer lurking mere feet away from where I sit. I am reassured and somehow disappointed at once as I go back to the film.

I recall that as a child, in the house in which all my dreams still take place, I would stay up on Friday night and watch the late-night scary movie. Vampires and zombies and two headed transplants would stalk across the screen before my young eyes, as I lay wrapped in a blanket on the floor in front of the television, with all the lights in the house extinguished, the glow from the box before me the only illumination.

At the conclusion of the movie, there would be a patriotic station sign off, with video of an Air Force pilot in flight and a voiceover reading from Magee's "High Flight" and then the screen would go to static.

And I would lay there, blanket pulled up to my chin, peering nervously around into the void of the living room, listening intently as the old house creakingly settled into the cool of the night. Gathering my courage to make the journey upstairs to my bed. After a little while, the gloom grew less opaque, and I could make out gradations in black and shadow, and forms materialized.

Invariably, at some point in this weekly ritual, I would look to the stairs, a dozen feet from where I lay, and I would see someone, something, a shape slowly gliding down them.

As I struggled to make out details, a ghostly face that I could only just discern would turn from the path it was taking down the stairway to fix its vacant gaze upon me, there on the floor.

This was the same malevolent entity, I imagined, that had followed me from another house in which we lived, where it dwelt in the attic, coming down to the door at night, a door adjacent to my childhood bedroom, to claw and rap at it while I lay frozen in my bed.

Now, I would watch my imagination's invention of the thing as it descended to join me, fairly quivering in anticipation, half terror, half excitement to discover that the mundane waking stage of sun and light was not the extent of our world. That there were dark crevices from which slithery things watched, places haunted by ghouls and shrouds that wanted commerce with us in life, the child's naïve desire for demons, so long as they can only spook and unsettle but not corrupt.

Sad, empty, incomplete, the adult world that destroys and cauterizes one's capacity for belief that things like that one I so regularly beheld as a boy could be and could come from some distant, icy void to waft down the stairway of the house I grew up in and fill me with that delicious dread that is inspired by the eerie fullness of the universe.

ON THE DENTIST'S CHAIR WITH A RADIO HIT OF 1978 IN HIS EARS

I CLIMBED INTO THE CHAIR WHILE the dental hygienist made small talk. How would human beings who did not know each other well ever be in the same space together without finding trivialities to discuss and without pretending that the trivialities they offered to one another were not trivialities, but vibrantly interesting insights into critically important matters?

"There's supposed to be some snow tonight."

Unbeknownst to me, she had made some version of this precise statement to every other person who had been seated in this chair before me today. Six times, to be precise.

I was aware of the game's rules even as I often failed in my adherence to them to effectively camouflage how aware I was that it was indeed a performance that was being undertaken on all sides.

"Oh yeah? I didn't hear about that. How much?"

"Oh, not too much, though it's going to be pretty cold!"

"Ah." I thought that had sounded too transparently uncommitted, and I hoped she would not notice.

She asked me what flavor I preferred for the tooth polish. Mint is always the safest option, so this was my choice. She seemed satisfied by my conservative decisiveness.

As she put the chair back, I wet my lips to be sure I would not split one of them during the extended period of sitting there with my mouth stretched wide open that was in the offing. The light above me shone directly into my eyes, and the gleam from the face shield she was wearing created an explosive effect, modulating, disappearing, reappearing in a different location every time she shifted her angle of vision slightly.

I thought about nothing in particular.

The effect of the double espresso I had before coming into the office was just settling in, intensified by the blood rushing to my head as the chair tilted me at an angle never approximated in everyday life.

The dentist's office PA system was tuned to some online seventies and eighties station. This, the music that had been on the radio in my youth, is now universally referred to as "Oldies." The music that made up the "Oldies" when I was a kid has unceremoniously disappeared from the public sphere. As a young man, going to a doctor's office or other place where background music could be expected meant hearing songs that evoked no meaningful personal memories. Now, I had become one of those people who had recurrent nostalgic episodes in elevators because music was constantly playing there that took me back to the Dairy Queen when I was fourteen, sharing a sundae with a blonde girl and listening to Elton John and the Bee Gees on the jukebox, or to hitting a game winning triple in Little League off the lanky kid who struck out everybody, and then hearing the radio in somebody's car after the game playing that song that could be heard every half hour on every FM station that summer.

Pop music is simple music in its composition. It is easy to ridicule if one has even the slightest degree of musical sophistication. And this is the easiest of things to do with the pop music of every generation that is not yours. But the stuff on the radio that was first captured by your auditory nerve and then transmitted to the neurons when your child's brain was still bursting in development, *that* simple music will forever have an emotional valence lacking in what your mother or your children listened to, which is for the musical elitist patently rubbish and amenable to eternal criticism in the interest of vigilance for Music, capital M.

For a child of the seventies, the Captain and Tennille, Boston, Starland Vocal Band, and the Bellamy Brothers are forever exempted from such aesthetic rigor. That music resides in some other place, far from the brain, the neurological facts notwithstanding, and much closer to the emotional center of being that is found behind the rib cage. Yes, yes, of course, technically, artistically, that decade's pop music was as worthless as that of the Archies or the Big Bopper or Katy Perry or Destiny's Child or Taylor Swift or Justin Bieber. *Of course.* But it would forever hit your brain differently than the trash that you had first heard as a forty year old, or that as a child you already knew as your parents' music, or that you had never troubled yourself to hear at all because you could not bear to pay even the slightest bit of attention to what thirteen year olds were listening to now.

In many cases, one does not even register the music of other generations as *music*, at least, one's brain refuses to do any of the work that would be necessary on hearing it to associate it with profound emotional chemistry and reaction. It strikes one in precisely the same way that traffic noise or incoherent yelling from another room in the same building might. Sound that registered as such, but without attracting real attention.

As I sat in the chair, or rather as I lay suspended upside down, I disappeared into a reverie.

Somehow, through the random chance of this series of neurons getting exercised by the combination of stimuli, the caffeine, the inverted chair that placed my head closer to the ground than my feet, I found myself thinking about the walk I made every day from my childhood home to the two schools I had attended from seventh grade through high school graduation. Not just abstractly but considering it in the finest detail. Precise images, maps of blocks and neighborhood features appeared in my mind. The two schools were within a few blocks of each other, so the walk was the same for six years. About two miles, one way. Thirty-five minutes or so. From High Street to 4th, down 4th to Frebis, then to Wilson, to Thurman and finally Ann Street. Street names that were recalled without effort, even with forty years separating me from the last time I had trod them.

A huge field of overgrown grass and weeds, with no houses or other buildings, right in the middle of an otherwise crowded neighborhood of working-class homes came to me. How many times had I walked past it? Two hundred days in a school year times six. I walked the same way there and back, so twice a day. Almost twenty-five hundred times I had walked that path, past that field, minus a few absences for illnesses and some snow days when school was cancelled, at a time in life when my mind was absorbing everything for storage and recall in unforeseen future circumstances.

I could see it in my mind's eye as though I were standing before it now, fifteen years old, fresh-souled, clear-eyed, certain that the horizon of life was wide and far, far away in the distance. I could see the wildflowers, the dandelions, the waist high grass here and there where it had not been trampled, the piles of dirt, the junk that had been dumped by people in the surrounding neighborhoods, bricks, some half-destroyed kitchen cabinets, a toilet, pieces of automobiles and numerous tires, the bike trails kids had left on their journeys through on high speed chases, the soda cans and the McDonalds bags and straws. I could see it all as vividly as I could see the exam light and the glare from the hygienist's face mask.

I would sometimes stop there on the way home, on warm days, and just sit. Climb up on a pile of dirt and sit there, like some out-of-time Stylite, meditating on the name of God on my mound while the world passed around me. Ferociously trying to dig through the illusion to the reality, to find the something I could not identify but the existence of which I was perpetually aware because of the gnawing, unceasing ache in my gut, the incompleteness. In my mind's eye, it was so present that I might have reached out to touch my youthful self, pensive there on his dirt heap, pondering everything and nothing. I might have touched him with a hand that was his own but separated by decades of future time.

"Everything looks good," I heard the dental hygienist say. "You can rinse with that cup of water. The dentist will be here in a minute to have a quick look." She hurried out of the room, leaving me alone with my vision.

I was absorbed by the image of myself, in a younger body, in the field. In the background, somewhere above him, I heard a voice.

"And it's taken you so long,

To find out you were wrong,

When you thought it held everything."

I listened. "Yes, it has," came the thought. "It has."

I thought of how, as a boy, I would sometimes climb out my window onto the roof at night and just sit there for hours, perched above the yard in the darkness. I had the impression then that I was dangling in the void, and all it would take was a relaxing of my posture to effect a drop into that black sea.

"You used to think that it was so easy," sang the voice.

There I was, at once the Buddha sitting zazen and a crouching bird of prey at the edge of the roof.

"Another year and then you'd be happy,

But you're cryin', you're cryin' now . . . "

It came as a flash, triggered by those sounds and those words, the banalities of my generation impervious to the immune response of my critical faculties, that my twelve year old ears had absorbed so many times at precisely the moment that the hormonal transformation was beginning in my body and I first began to think about the world beyond childhood, however furtively and murkily.

Perhaps the melancholy way that melody and that lyric, not even maudlin to the serious musician, hit my pristine consciousness, still uncluttered by sophistication, in that time now so distant had left a trace that the years and the accumulation of knowledge about the arrangement of sound could not erase. Neurons are not replaced; they last until you die. Those neurons that had been imprinted with emotional experiences, now unavailable to my memory, seasoned by that song may still have retained the same configuration of connections through the decades. They were unchanged by the accretion of other experiences. They insisted on moving me in a way that better music, learned later, could never hope to do.

"Another year and then you'd be happy,

But you're cryin', you're cryin' now . . . "

Something happened. To turn it into words is already to distort it into something else. But without the need for words, or even for a silent narrative inside my head, a realization was made.

The voice inside my head that did not have to speak said this:

"I do not care at all if I am dead in a month. Why should I? That is not real. The idea of being dead in a month is nothing but an idea. It is no more real than the idea of the day the sun goes supernova and engulfs every planet in the solar system, including Earth, in a glorious, destructive wave of celestial funeral plasma. What is real is one thing, one thing only: This moment right now, when you are alive. It is all there is. All of it. What is to be worried about? How can one be frightened of what is not in the all? How can one be frightened of what is not? Here you sit, thinking these thoughts, seeing these images in the mind emanating from the brain in your head that is functioning perfectly well, at this moment, right now. Here you are. This is it. There is nothing else."

The song went into the bridge, then back for the final verse. Tears welled up in my eyes as I listened.

One of my dead sisters' faces came to me, then the second. They were singing the chorus, from somewhere I could not name. The beloved ones, gone, taken away from me by brutal destiny, had come back to press the point. Here you are. This is it. Nothing else. Just this. Be here. Nothing else. Just be here, and everything is okay. There is nothing not here right now that is part of the conversation about what is okay or not okay, nothing to worry about trying to make okay at some later point or to keep okay beyond this moment. There is just this. The only thing there is, the only thing you have, the only thing you can ever have. You have already arrived. You are already home, and home is wherever you are right now, in all the nows of however much time you get to be a breathing bundle of living cells.

This, I now knew, in a way I had never known before, though I had read all the right books and could recite all the tidbits of philosophy that would indicate how aware of all the meaningful things I must be, this was the same experience Siddhartha Gautama had sitting beneath the Bodhi Tree. The same experience had by the student in the koan, chased away with a stick by the master with whom he had wished to study wisdom. The same experience of Saul on the road to Damascus. The same experience of Muhammad in the cave on Jabal al-Nour.

Not a similar experience. The same one. Precisely the same. This moment was the same moment those others lived. An eternal light shining from a pristine black sky, illuminating everything, the backdrop of dark somehow both obliterated and enhanced for relief against the purity of realization.

The dentist came into the room to find me wiping my eyes and laughing.

NIGHT FLIGHT

FOUR OR FIVE TEEN MALES of the species, wild in the bush, formidable animals drawn to risk and danger. My tribe, my pack, my troop. We are full of spit, fire, and trouble, eager for an opportunity to spend our excess energy, to show the world, and ourselves, that we are specimens to be reckoned with, dangerous, for real.

A taste of alcohol and the transgressive intoxication it delivers are what we want, but we are working class boys, and we have no money. For those of our breed, though, this is of no moment. It is the thrill of stepping over lines, of breaking rules that we are after, and that, like the beer, can be had for free, with a little luck. And without the luck, the price will be steeper.

Our technique is as unsophisticated as our reasoning about the possible consequences of our planned actions. Walk into the carry-out. The beer display is right there near the door. Cartons of 24 cans stacked in a mountain several feet high and twice as wide. Nervous whispered conversation of five or ten seconds, the mere figment of a plan, but we all know it is pure improvisation from here, bravado and speed. There are five more friends waiting for us at the house nearby. We have only to make it to the car.

One carton each. Single file, pick up, walk calmly toward the cashier. Expressions that give nothing away, as stealth is our only weapon, non-violent delinquents that we are, and we would likely just drop the goods and run if offered any resistance. Avoid looking directly at the register clerk as we approach, the feigned inattention of the lawful, then just keep going. Break for the door and keep going right through it and out into the parking lot and then accelerate as the clerk realizes what is happening and yells "Hey, what the hell are you doing?!" Too late.

We hit the pavement at full sprint. We are young and we run fast and well.

But as we reach the sidewalk, a curveball from the Fates. A cruiser pulls into the lot, a random accident for the purpose of our work, but one with potentially catastrophic consequences. Cosmic justice perhaps asserting its disdain for having been so rudely ignored.

It will take the cop a few seconds to get inside the store and be informed by the clerk, and by then we are away, for the moment at least, scattered into the night. A block's distance from the carry-out, the waiting car collects us. We let them know the story, laughing hysterically but nervously. We hide the beer in the trunk and get back out, knowing the car is likely to be stopped before it makes it home. With nervous confidence, we tell them we will see them soon.

What had gone before, it turns out, was not the game. Now, the true game is on.

Off the road, we head to the railroad track running along the river. The squad cars cannot reach us there. We are already cackling in triumph, though not yet at all sure how this will end, when we hear the police helicopter overhead.

They called out a helicopter for a $50 beer run?

We duck like the seasoned criminals we are pretending to be into the trees, wait for it to pass overhead, then back to the tracks to run along them crazily until we hear the 'copter again, then we return to the trees, large, clothed rabbits bolting from hedge to hedge to avoid the metallic hawk. We were talking before, joking, laughing. All that piss and vinegar has run out of us now. We are scared shitless, silent and assiduous about the effort to avoid capture and the rest of what that would entail.

As I run, and the helicopter's sound and light hover now at the rim of my perception and now pass above in a rush, movie and TV police chases I have seen flit through my brain. We have leapt off the screen, and we exist now in flesh and sweat and hearts pounding with exertion and fear.

I imagine we must be giving off a glow. The aura that things of myth always exude. I am at once burning up and chilled with fiery exultation of my will's command of the world and ice-cold fear that I have ruined my life for something trivial.

It is nearly an hour before we arrive, our journey made incalculably circuitous first by the sight and sound of cruisers and helicopter, then by our paranoia that the emergent silence means we should detour into this alley and then that in order to avoid the pursuers we cannot see but sense must be just up ahead. We are caked with mud, dead tired, still more than a little worried that the police will pop up just before we get in the door, but exhilarated.

We learn our intuition was accurate. The car was stopped, but the clerk could not identify those in it as the ones in the store, so they were left to bring our well-hidden booty back to wait on us.

Celebration of youthful transgression and the fact that it is still possible to escape from the grip of power and do what you will, or at least to imagine you have done so. It might well have been mead from the halls of the gods that we deliriously poured down our throats, chortling, choking with joyful triumph, giddy, thrilled to be here, a band of brothers, together and not in the back of a squad car or in jail but free, and to have won, to have won, just this once, and even with so paltry a reward.

Two of my brethren from that night were gone from this veil within but a few years, other risks, still greater, run and lost.

The gambler's life. Only the one who gives it up in time gets the chance to think fondly back on it later.

CONSUMING FLESH

IT IS NEVER A MUNDANE ACT. That we do not remember is our own shame and our loss.

Spirits were extinguished so that you could imbibe the frames they inhabited.

Yes, it has been bowdlerized beyond recognition, and the people who most claim it are frequently those one does not want as allies. But the invocation of the spirit animal, the humble request, the promise to repay and to do well with the sustenance, all this was present in some cultures, those too close to the earth to survive in competition with others who built superior killing machines.

We mastered them there, but they are our betters here, and that we do not even recognize it is the revelation of the distance between us in that ranking.

The texture, the smell, the plenitude of every morsel of flesh. Fat, blood, sinew, bone, sliced, chopped, broiled, seared, taken raw, I savor every speck of this precious, beautiful, irreplaceable being whose life is given for mine.

This annihilation that makes an empty space that I fill with my expanded energy and vitality.

Thank you, spirit, for this unfathomably valuable gift, which you did not give of your own will, which was taken by assertive and violent force, but which I am nevertheless obligated to acknowledge if I would stay in balance with the world's calculus.

The communion of it, the sacrifice, the holiness, the gift of this one whose lifeblood now is metabolically made into my skin, my eyes, my muscles, my heart, my thoughts, and my very soul.

In every human society, meat is preferred over all other foods. In every single one.

How did we, in our modern insanity, find a way to create people who not only abstain from the sacred *fête* themselves but seek, with anemic moralities, to prevent other celebrants from worshipping at the communal plate?

Our primate relatives—the chimps, the baboons—they hunt too, and they kill, and they partake. And their females favor the males who hunt well and provide them with bellies full of monkey or gazelle flesh.

The primordial truth of the flesh, of the blood. No lie can alter it.

In death, life. In life, death.

THREE CINEMA FACES

HARRIET ANDERSSON IN
SMILES OF A SUMMER NIGHT

Petra, the beautiful house servant, answers the door as the lawyer Egerman and his wife return from the play.

She smiles radiantly in asking them, surprised, if the play has already ended, and at the end of the phrase, her expression subtly transforms from the smile to something indescribably lovely. The doting look of the servant girl, waiting on instructions from her master, with the innocence of the young virgin, and the shame of the unexpected shock of finding them there at that hour, as she had a moment earlier been inside toying with the feeble efforts at courtship of the lawyer's son.

Interrupted in their little tryst, she converts instantly from the alluring erotic tart to the bashful, pristine girl unsullied by anything so sultry.

What on this earth could be more breathtakingly beautiful than the passing of this expression over that beatific visage?

In another scene, the socially climbing Petra again works at the seduction of the pathetic son, who is enthralled by her loveliness, just as the rest of us. She walks into the room where he is having breakfast alone, sets a vase of flowers down on the table, playfully blows in his ear and walks provocatively around the table. She turns her back and undoes her top, turns back to him with her breast exposed and a heavenly smile on her lips, takes his hand to place it on her breast. In that instant she changes her expression to the same innocent, half-surprised look from the earlier scene.

Magical, pure and impure moments of aesthetic perfection.

⌇

ELISABETH SHUE IN *LEAVING LAS VEGAS*

She is talking to an analyst about her relationship with the Nicolas Cage character.

"No, I don't think I should see him again . . . but I look for him. I went . . . out last night, I was looking for him."

The exquisite complexity of emotional range she shows in these few bare seconds:

- from *"No"* (with the nervous exhalation of breath at the end of this utterance, her face is that of a little girl who has been caught pilfering cookies and sheepishly admits to it, then a rebellious smile and the mischievous laugh confirming her enjoyment of this transgressive desire);

- to *"I don't think I should see him again"* (her face sets sternly for a moment in recognition of the danger, and then eyebrows arch to show innocent repentance, seeking the questioner's acknowledgement of her confession of her sin);

- and then, she looks down momentarily, and, abruptly, *"but I look for him"* (a wisp of a laugh at *"but"*, and a voluptuous smile when the phrase is completed, her eyes sparkling with unadulterated bliss at the mere thought of this man she already loves, and again a hint of that rebellion);

- and finally *"I went . . . out last night, I was looking for him"* (she shakes her head at *"went"*, as if to clear the intoxication of the thought of him from her mind, and her voice is nearly trembling with excitement as she finishes the phrase, looking down, ashamed to show her abandon to this person she knows cannot approve of what she cannot escape feeling).

A lengthy novel could be written about just what her face conveys in this scene and never approach its depth.

~

LIV ULLMANN IN *SHAME*

As she and Max von Sydow drive to the ferry, he speaks to her as she is about to exit the car to open the gate.

They have nearly had an argument. But he tells her that when he saw her, just a minute before, buying fish from a local fisherman at the creek, he felt great love for her, as she was so beautiful at that moment.

Her placid face instantly warms. She breaks into a shy smile, her delicately pale, deeply freckled complexion lit spectacularly by the sunshine through the windshield.

She gets out of the car, looks in at him through the passenger window as the sunlight streams across her glowing face, goes to open the gate, gets back into the car, beams at him again and kisses him.

The sheer Nordic contour of her face, the angles, the inward curve of the line of her nose, that alabaster skin with its intimate texture visible by the grace of this miraculous light that Sven Nykvist was able to conjure, alone of all cinematographers.

The camera is behind them in the car, and it follows her as she goes around the front of it to the gate, beams at von Sydow again in the driver side window as he pulls through, then comes around the back to enter the car again.

Breathtaking archetypal physiognomy of love.

PIGEONS

A BENCH IN A PARK, SOMEWHERE in a city of a summer. A few inches of leftover bread after a mobile lunch.

Before I go, I decide to give the bread to the mass of pigeons that have been watching me greedily, keeping a safe distance so long as I have the baguette near my mouth, cautiously moving in when they see it go down onto the bench beside me.

I tear it into chunks and throw them into the crowd of birds. All the struggle of nature instantly manifests, right here before me, in this mundane public square.

I give many crumbs at a time, so more than just the largest few can feed. But no matter how I make the division, the squabbling and merciless contestation is omnipresent. The stronger, faster, and bolder chase off the others, or simply take the bread directly from their beaks.

It is pristinely simple, the rule that motivates all that happens here, and a little reflection reveals that this is the same rule everywhere.

Because we humans have amended the rule, however imperfectly, to at least occasionally reduce its brutality, I find it hard to accept that the pigeons handle their business in this atrocious manner. I try to legislate, fool that I am, caught up in my cultural game of fairness and equity and sharing and other such notions. I go as far as to give crumbs to weaker birds and then to stand between them and their larger antagonists. I chase away the most aggressive birds.

But they return immediately as soon as I retreat or when they sense that I am too focused on some other aggressor to attend to them. Even as I endeavor to isolate the smaller birds in order to feed them, the once victims spontaneously convert to victimizers and begin bullying one another, and a new hierarchy of power is imposed that is the perfect copy with different participants of the hierarchy I disrupted.

My efforts prove without results, or in any event the results I hoped to achieve are not produced. The pigeons are uninterested in my prejudices. They prefer their own.

Might and aggression mixed with some luck gets a bit of bread, weakness and pacifism only and always starves.

Cold, pure, uncompromising, utterly separated from the world hairless apes have devised out of our ability to produce sounds and then etch symbols representing the sounds on parchment and then name some among us as the guardians of these sacred symbols that we desire so desperately to be eternal rules for the governing of our commerce with one another.

As the pigeons continue their war of all against all, I notice something I had not seen before.

There are three or four dozen birds gathered around the bench, hard to count as they bustle about in the furious competition like balls of feathers in the wind. Of all the birds I study to verify the point, not a single one has two intact feet.

All are missing toes or have other horrible deformities. Some have no foot at all on one leg, just a stump. These hobble about pathetically, yet impervious to my compassion for them. They feed when I give them the opportunity to do so by intimidating their intimidators, and then they adopt the same amoral rigor in their competition with still smaller, weaker, more severely crippled fellows. My pity for their condition plays precisely no role in the mechanism of the malevolent machinery.

I return to my bench, thoroughly defeated. It is difficult to look hard at such things. Doing so inevitably reminds one of how much of this is contained in us too.

CONTACT

I HAD, FOR THE FIRST TIME in my life, arrived too early at the airport. The late and the barely punctual were bustling and pushing to get somewhere quickly all around me, and I sat calmly, pristinely, in a situation with which I was wholly unfamiliar. I tried to read, but the lone cup of coffee I had poured down my throat had been an insufficient jolt to the system and my attention could not be focused. I walked around, looking with little hope for a seat that had no spilled liquid or wad of chewing gum or human occupant in it.

Flight 484 from Leipzig was arriving. Maybe it was 494. The announcements were barely discernible above the din of the other creatures who were there with me in this absurdly large enclosure, this cage for animals not favored by natural selection with wings but only with enough neurons and synapses to invent flying machines. I was not hungry, but I decided to spend the last coins in my pocket before boarding, so I stuck them into a vending machine. Pushed a few buttons. There was a brief noise, then the little arm stopped moving short of reaching its destination in front of the chocolate bar I had selected. I pushed the button again, to no effect.

The dark-haired woman in her mid-20s who was at the counter just to the right of the vending machine had seen the whole thing. She solicitously came to me and asked what happened, then pushed the buttons again in my stead. She was met with the same robotic disdain. She fetched for me from her register the same amount in coins I had wished to lose. Her smile was more than worth the return of what I only wanted to give away.

After I found my seat on the plane, I tried the book again, with more success. It looked as though I would have the aisle to my-self until just a few minutes before takeoff. Then a young woman walked up and took the seat to my immediate left. She had long, straight hair, very light skin, greenish eyes. She was wearing some perfume that I vaguely recognized, berries and vanilla and other scents I could not identify but nonetheless knew. She did not look at me as she took her seat.

As I buckled my seatbelt, I inadvertently bumped her arm, lightly, and begged her pardon. She did not speak, only smiling wanly and nodding her head while her eyes met mine fleetingly and then returned to their previous focus elsewhere. "Is the next stop home, or are you connecting to somewhere else?" I asked. She said she had another plane to catch once they arrived that would take her to the city where she was studying. What was she studying? Business. Some kind of exchange program. It was clear by her demeanor that this was to be the limit of our conversation. I understood it was best to return to the book, which was after all not so bad, and so I did.

It was an eight-hour flight.

Many other things happened between this brief exchange and the pilot's announcement that arrival was imminent. Children ran in the aisles while their parents slept. There was entertainment on the screens in the seatbacks. Food was served twice, drinks three times, trash collected, forms filled out. My legs ached at one point, and I asked her if I might pass to get to the aisle. She wordlessly obliged.

The descent to the airport commenced. I buckled my seat belt and put my book away. Thought of the task of finding my way to the baggage claim area and then ground transportation. Mundanity. A way to avoid thinking of the fact that taking off and landing are the two most dangerous times in an airplane.

The earth approached rapidly.

The landing gear banged on the runway once, then the plane went up again, then down, then up again. Then a third time the tires thumped against the ground, and the plane swerved slightly to the right. The pilot did something to correct for the slide, and this caused the plane to tilt in the other direction, so precipitously that one of the landing wheels left the ground altogether.

A collective gasp was emitted by some quantity of the passengers, immediately punctuated by shouts and screams, as that single datum no one on a plane wants demonstrated to them became clear: *Something was not going as planned and this was potentially of the most dire nature imaginable.*

There was a terrible scraping sound, thunderously loud, and a concomitant shuddering felt through the cabin as the tip of the left wing touched the runway in a shower of sparks.

I had no time for a coherent thought during all of this. There was only a flickering memory of my childhood. There I was on a Big Wheel, the plastic front wheel so brutalized by high-speed stops that it had flattened out in several places, flying down the sidewalk in front of an apartment in which my parents and I had lived for a few months during the year I was in kindergarten.

This idyllic snatch of mental video had never previously appeared to me, at least not in waking adulthood, and it is a mystery of the universe why it did so now.

As the Big Wheel and the sidewalk were flickering out as quickly as they had been illuminated, the right arm of the young business student shot out and wrapped itself tightly around my left upper arm, her left hand extended over her body and grabbed my upper left thigh, and her whole body leaned over in the seat to pull the two of us into a tight embrace. She whimpered in fear and put her head on my shoulder. It rested there for perhaps five seconds. The smell of her shampoo wafted to my nostrils.

An eternity passed through my consciousness.

Then the plane straightened, dropped down again onto all three wheels, and braked hard. The pilot had regained control. We were safe.

She released her grip and sat back up straight in her seat. She was breathing heavily but otherwise looked exactly as she had in the instant before the near catastrophe began.

She did not look at me but fixed her gaze on the seatback in front of her. The danger past, the commotion in the plane ceased, and all reverted to the silent, courteous isolation of modern human existence.

Soon, the plane came to a stop. The pilot said something over the PA that I did not hear. The passengers all gathered our things and exited dully.

Her eyes met mine for a split second, one final time, as she picked up her bag and made to walk down the aisle toward the cockpit, and toward the airport and her next flight and the rest of her life.

I stayed in my seat until all the other passengers had left, staring straight ahead, trying to hold on to something unnamed that was already disappearing. Then I too wordlessly took up my earthly belongings and exited the plane.

PHIL AND HIS GUITAR

MY FRIEND DIED IN HIS WHITE Ford Econoline van of a heroin overdose thirty years ago.

He was found in the morning in the driver's seat, the vehicle out of gas. He just did a little more than he could handle. He had been off the stuff for a while, then gone back on. He might have forgotten how much was just enough and how much was too much. Gotten overconfident about his capacity. Does one ever know exactly where that line is, with respect to anything? With respect to heroin, you frequently get no free mistakes.

He wrote me some tearfully funny cards from San Francisco when he was living in a flophouse out there, trying to play music. The cards were funny even though they were sometimes about topics that are not supposed to be funny. Drugs and street crime and living in this hard world and the sadness and suffering it entails.

When I heard he was dead—it was his dear mother who told me—I wondered how it could be so. I did not doubt that it was possible. He was after all living as a transient in a strange city, and in a dangerous relationship with a dangerous substance, with no family or friends within hundreds of miles of him. But it was still too much to believe it had really happened.

I knew death. People I love had gone away from me into that realm already, so it was not a stranger. Yet when I heard about Phil, I sat at the table and looked at nothing and unsuccessfully tried to gather it in. To come to grips with the fact that here it was, cold, brute, unyielding, and ever and always unchangeable.

~

Phil played guitar.

That is not quite right. He did not do anything so mundane. Anyone who knows a G-major chord can play a guitar, technically speaking. You can learn that in five minutes, even if it takes a bit longer to commit it to muscle memory and grow the calluses that dull the pain of the strings. Phil did not merely play guitar. What he did was to coax the guitar through some process opaque to me to produce music, somehow, unfathomably, mysteriously, supernaturally. He inhabited it in some way so as to make it part of him, him part of it, and it and he made sound together in that hybrid state.

I have never heard anyone else get a guitar to do what Phil could get a guitar to do. And I have heard all the great guitar players. All the ones you might name for me, I am fairly sure I know them. I have heard them, on their records, and some in person. I have known a few people with superb training on guitar, who could work many wonderful and astounding miracles with the instrument. So far as I know, Phil had little or no formal training. He had only him, the force that was him, and that is all he brought to bear on the task.

To think of him is to think of that noise that he managed to make emerge from that guitar and that amplifier.

We made music together for a time. I struck and tapped and attacked various objects percussively. He picked up his guitar and plugged it in and made it sing its extraordinary song. We did this at the same time, in the same place, together.

Those moments, just he and I in a room alone, two souls separated from the human sea, without preconceived plans, just sitting down with our tools and fixing our minds on the common good, on the beautiful, terrifying, pristine, sacrosanct place toward which we were attempting to set sail, collectively, I and he, the two of us, engaged, heightened, attuned, paying attention, attention, attention, listening, he to me, I to him, each to the other.

Making music together.

Communicating with sounds that are not words, that exceed language, that transcend the prosaic humdrum of that quotidian interactional game and enter another, more rarefied space.

Have I ever been more alive than in those moments I shared with him?

We sometimes thought it was rubbish, what we had done on a particular day, then we listened to the recording, and we would sit silent, hushed, worshipful, ashamed by our lack of faith. Other times we thought we had done well, and then listened again, and looked immediately at one another, my eyes into his, his into mine, and it was understood, we had been misled this time, and we would have to try again.

But back to it we would go. Eager, full of anticipation, if also with trepidation, for we were invoking gods and powers beyond us, we would go down to the basement and turn on all the switches and knobs, and say our inward prayers, and strive to get outside ego and let music speak through us.

Our audience was the two of us. Him. Me. No one else. We cared not a whit for the opinions of anyone else, even if what we were doing was preparation for the presentation of our collective enterprise to others at a later time. This cannot be stressed enough. The matter of what others might think about what we had made never even occurred to us. We assumed as a certainty that once we were happy with our ability to produce interesting performances on more or less any given occasion that we sat down together to do so, there would be others who would be interested in what we considered interesting. We never played the recordings for anyone else. Obviously, we reasoned, no one who was not present could have a meaningful perspective on what we had done, and we two were always, always the only ones.

We only talked about music if it could not be avoided and for as little time as absolutely necessary to communicate whatever practical thing needed communicating.

Just play. Let the music be.

How I loved him. How much I loved him. My dear, dear brother.

He was so difficult. Impossible, even. Often unlovable. But nevertheless, no matter, despite it all, because of what we shared, how I loved him.

～

What I felt on hearing of his death was that I no longer had the right to sit on my ass and try to have a normal life. That is what I felt, immediately, like a wound, like a punch in the face, like a thunderclap.

Wake up. Now.

Phil had gently and not so gently prodded me about this for years. Do something, get something accomplished, something that makes the suffering bearable. When we were not in the same place, he would write me those postcards, with hilarious scribbled drawings on one side and on the other some economically expressed version of *"You Have Something to Say. Say It Before It Is Too Late."*

I listened sometimes, for a little while, and went to work, trying to figure out how to let the spirit flow out, how to shamanically go alone to that place he and I had often frequented together and to open up enough of a door between there and here to let that energy flow into this world in some way.

But then the whirlwind of everyday life and concerns and stresses and responsibilities and all of that tediousness drowned out his voice in my brain.

Now I would have to listen to him because he was no longer and to ignore him now was an affront even I, in my carelessness, in my laziness, could not countenance.

And yet the time passed, and his death receded toward some horizon, and there were other things that had to be done, and I did not heed what he told me in his absence, and so it was and so it is and so it will be.

Would he be surprised by that failure? Saddened? Understanding? Would he know that what we did, the places we went, would he understand that they required us both, and that they are now lost, and that they will never ever return, and that this is the everything of their sacred power?

Yes. He would know.

VERA C.

EUCALYPTUS TREES ARE NATIVE TO AUSTRALIA, but they had been transplanted somehow, through a complexity of the world's movements and transmigrations, to this place on the other side of the world where I found myself in the southern California sun.

I had never seen them in my life until I lived here. They whispered outside my window in the early morning hours, telling tales of the unfathomably ancient that I only half-heard as I sat absorbed in a song, two and half minutes of pristine sonic truth and beauty that I played over and over, until the dawn came to draw me finally to sleep, and to dreams populated by all things vanished and mourned.

A simple set of chords from an acoustic guitar, austerity itself. It was for me a meditation on an essential part of my life and my world that I feared had been doomed by the Fates, now the dust of memory alone.

Listening to those chords, death encircles me, but it is somehow warm, enchantingly recalling the glow of the departed. The death of the life I lived when I first discovered that music, now more than a quarter century away, and the passing of a passionate love that I swore was eternal as it burned itself into my soul and that now lies still in the grave of the past, yet another precious thing gone that I believed eternal.

And death too in the disappearance of the man who wrote the music, who perished some years ago, his music now propelled only by those who still people this world. I, the others, few as they are, who sell and buy his recordings or put them on the Internet where others still alive can hear them, all of us, each one of us, ourselves counting out the seconds until our own untimely end.

For all endings, no matter how much they have been anticipated with hushed reverence, are thus: *Untimely.*

This music bears a woman's name.

Vera C.

I do not know who she was, or is, and I likely never will. The song is too obscure to have made a significant imprint on the interconnected web of data servers that are the basis of human knowledge at present. I search for her and find only an astronomer named Vera C. Rubin, who has an observatory in Chile named for her.

Could the Vera C. of this music still be alive? How could I discover this fact without expending time and energy I do not have, tracking down the composer's colleagues and associates to ask them about the mysterious woman I have created behind this haunting music? And for what? To be given mundane facts from reality which can never measure up to the pristine fantasy I have created for myself about her.

My Vera C. is a melancholy French Algerian, with the same mouth and nose as Isabelle Adjani, raven dark hair, a gaze that tells of sadness without end borne with stoic diffidence.

She has hands and fingers so delicate you fear merely stroking or holding them would cause her physical injury, so you struggle against the overwhelming urge to hold to her as though she were life itself.

Her only physical flaw, which she hides as she talks with those thin hands and which is only visible when she laughs, is the stained rear teeth from the administration of tetracycline when she was a young girl suffering from chronic illness.

It is this one flaw however that is also the gift that brought her to me, as it produced in her the profoundly sad longing for another time and place that is precisely what drew the musician to her, led him to become her friend, to desire to be her lover without ever finding the way to make this come to pass, and eventually inspired him to compose this delicate ghost, this funereal shroud of a song for her.

Perhaps he wrote the song after noting the look in her eye at the moment he imagined her to be thinking about her own death.

The Vera C. of this flitting shadow moment, she too is dead, whether she still walks the planet somewhere or not.

The original version of the song, the naked version, is only the acoustic guitar and, entering midway through, an accompaniment of strings, but there exists a more embellished version with additional instrumentation and vocals. In this version, a female voice mellifluously calls in Spanish: "Yo no quiero nada . . . " She is anticipating the catastrophe she cannot escape, relinquishing her claim to anything as an embrace of the diamond-hard hopelessness that is the human condition without faith.

Sometimes I would play the whole LP side and wait impatiently for her to arrive at the end, everything before that the most delicious anticipation. Other times I went right to the song and played it over and over until the hold of sleep became inescapable. Sitting into the wee hours, dreaming while awake. A phantasmal woman was reading in the other room, then sleeping. Cats lay on the couch and watched me disdainfully.

I had just at that time met a new friend. Together, we read Situationism and dreamed of kidnapping works of art from museums and holding them hostage. We pasted signs all over campus, alerting our fellows about the cages that were their everyday lives.

The irresistibly naïve young person's idea of overthrowing everything established and being unbearably cool in doing it. *Détourned* Archie comics on bright red paper with Sharpied political word balloons.

One of our posters was still there fifteen years later when I returned.

To see and converse with the ghosts.

And to look for Vera C.

LES PLEUREUSES

THE WEEPING WOMAN.

A funeral monument featuring a stone or bronze representation of a beautiful woman, often sitting or lying directly atop the burial site, tearfully mourning the passing of the one laid to rest inside.

~

She sometimes looks as if she is embracing the tomb, covered in a gauzy veil revealing the graceful shape of her hips, stomach, and breast.

Or she might be coiled fetally, her face turned to the side to show her agonized features, her lithe arms before her, the fingers of her hands interlaced delicately and resting on the tomb, in a sublime gesture of broken-hearted prayer.

She is sometimes greenish in hue, her bronze form oxidized by more than a century's exposure to the merciless elements.

The perfect line of her upper arm, and the mesmerizing purity of her neck and shoulders, the curve of her hip and the wave of her hair, so faultlessly reproducing the contours of the female form.

Her feet and toes so painstakingly rendered that you have to shake your head from time to time to break the illusion that she might at some point pause her inconsolable lament and sit up to catch her breath, just for a moment, before returning to the sacred rite she performs. How is she not alive? Did I not just hear her sob?

Sometimes, the *pleureuse* is not human but angelic, descending to the tomb from the heavens above, her gaze at once austere and maternal, perched watchfully here to attend to her dual task of mourning the dead and aiding the transport of his soul to the awaiting destination.

She adoringly puts the finishing touches on the stone's etching, or perhaps she is patiently waiting to add the names of the deceased's family members who will eventually come to reside here, her back and arms exotically streaked by the rains and snows of the years, and her noble gaze forever and lovingly fixed on the stone that will mark the site wherein their mortal forms rejoin the earth.

The singer Dalida became, at her suicide in 1987, her own magnificently modern yet still traditionally ethereal *pleureuse*, cheating the Reaper to stand radiantly, regally, eternally over the spot where her charnel remains lie. Bolts of light streak forth from behind her, her youth and beauty preserved for as long as stone lasts.

All, anything, the greatest failure imaginable could be redeemed fully and utterly, and a sullied life could be made holy by such a woman weeping at the death of the failed man.

The most ludicrous fool, I am convinced, the most unfortunate and inconsequential wastrel could be raised to the level of the gods by a *pleureuse* of sufficient spiritual purity and deathless pulchritude.

TRANSITION: SATURDAY, AUGUST 31, 1996

I WENT OUT ON THE TOWN with my friend.

First to a wine-soaked dinner at an Indian place, then to a party at the beach overpopulated with southern California yuppies, then finally to a filthy dirty hipster bar where I sat in a cloud of smoke and watched young people with facial piercings mill about tragically while listening to Red Hot Chili Peppers on the jukebox.

The alcohol level in my brain from dinner had been only mildly augmented at the party, as I was mindful of getting sick, and I had effectively regained my normal consciousness by the time we reached the bar. Rudely interrupted on the way to being pleasantly drunk and abruptly too aware of where I was and who surrounded me, I was growing bored and irritable by that time. My friend was intensifying the crisis by continuing to drink heavily and entering rant and rave mode.

Ranting and raving is less interesting when one is not oneself ranting or raving, even if the one ranting and raving is a close friend. I cannot remember what we were talking about. I no longer even remember why I refused to join him in pouring more down my gullet. A hopeless sense that the moment was gone and it was too late for all that.

A supremely frustrating experience, that of achieving slight drunkenness, and glimpsing the ecstatic merriment to come with greater intoxication, then realizing that the night is too early for continued heavy drinking, and so, with a reasonable eye toward avoiding an end to the night hovering over a toilet bowl, abstaining to buy some time, but then waiting too long and completely losing the buzz, and not even managing to find the desire to regain it because of an acute realization of the absurd emptiness of all of it.

As we exited the club at closing time and I waited on my friend to make the decision to finally call it a night, I stood stupidly watching the strange wave of humanity pour out the doors. I simply wanted to be someone and somewhere else more desperately than I could remember ever wanting it prior to that moment.

And then a beautiful young woman with a pierced navel appeared and somehow she was talking to us. You notice that immediately, the pierced navel. It tells you things about her that cannot be communicated any other way. A ravishing goddess—a Greek one, it turned out—who cast a spell with her very presence, speaking quickly and animatedly, yet giving off a glow of slow feminine heat and confidence.

She, I, my friend, and her two friends spoke for half an hour or so there, on the sidewalk just outside the now-closed bar, about movies, then her two friends departed and the goddess needed a ride home. She was going to 30th and University, and this just happened to be on our route, and my friend and I gave the goddess a ride to her place.

Throughout the six or seven minutes in my friend's pickup truck, she seated between us, her perfume having done the Dionysian work on me that I had refused to let wine do, I thought desperately of how I was going to see her again. I felt for an instant as though the Fates would work this out for me, as they had thrown her before me at the end of this night of revelry that had gone so wrong. Then the truck stopped, and time was up. I made an ill-conceived attempt, so awkward that to recall it today brings the blood to my cheeks, to get her to come with me to a movie at the local artsy cinema. She parried it easily, expertly, and then she was gone.

My friend dropped me at my apartment, mercifully not mentioning the spectacular nature of my defeat. I glanced at the clock, which read 3:38 a.m. I thought for fifteen minutes about the gleefully wicked games destiny plays with us, then I collapsed into slumber, to wake three hours later in a haze and walk down to the grocery store to gather boxes for packing books. I was moving out of the country in only a few days.

There was still hope.

EIGHT YEARS BEFORE
YOU WERE BORN, CHILD

EIGHT YEARS BEFORE YOU WERE born, child, to the month, perhaps to the very day of that month, though my imprecise journal note from the time does not allow such precision. In the fall of a year just a few before the millennium's end, that is when it happened.

I had no inkling then, of course, that you would come. As I wandered the streets of a foreign city, alone and seeking a companion, I could not know that you and I were planned by the secret weavers of lives.

I left a note for Frédéric Chopin, asking him to make me loved by my object of affection. I was told this was a thing one did, though it frankly did not make a lot of sense to me. Chopin had hardly been lucky in the game of love. Nonetheless, eager to adhere to the rituals of my adopted culture, I carefully crafted the letter, in French, and took it to his grave. I wish I had preserved the composition of the text, but that too is lost to time.

I waited impatiently for several other visitors to clear out, and then I affixed it with a stone, said an improvised prayer, and hurried out of the cemetery to have lunch at a café nearby. I listened with focused attention to some of his music for a few days afterward in an aural addition to the ritual. I recall especially pensively meditating over the Sonata in B-flat minor.

But within a week, I was certain that Chopin had paid my note no attention.

The one with whom I had asked him to intervene went about her business unperturbed, and I was to be no part of it. For a short while, it pained me, and I grieved, but then the busy pace of life washed over me. I let it be. With the passing of a few years, I had almost forgotten it entirely.

And then, still more years on, I met the one for whom I had all unknowing been waiting, and after a time you pierced the vale from the unseen world to this one and graced us with your presence, in a tearful miracle that for me will forever separate the before and the after of my existence.

You grew and you explored the world. You came to share my love of music. You asked me to teach you to play piano because you wanted to one day play Chopin, who moved you in the way he had moved me all those years ago.

Did he know? Did he grant my wish in a way that I could not comprehend, a way that I thought was a rejection or a silence in the face of my request? Was I, without knowing it, in a coded language indecipherable to the speaker, asking him to give me another love, a higher love, the love of a child then unknown and unknowable, one who would not be born for nearly another decade? One who would be with me forever, with my eyes and my temper and my blood and my soul?

THE ARCHIVES

IN A FOREIGN COUNTRY, WHERE the language is not my own, I am working in an old building undergoing renovation, metal shelving and exposed wiring all around me.

The room in which I sit is the reading room of an archive, and I am going through scads of correspondence and notes left by various writers from a hundred years ago to try to find useful things for a doctoral thesis. The boxes of old pages and folders and notebooks are delivered to me from a vast reserve somewhere in the bowels of the place, outside the gaze of mortals such as myself. Once they are placed on the desk, the emissary who fetched them speedily retreats to the unseen realm, and I am alone except for a secretary sitting on the other side of the room who never even glances in my direction, her gaze focused rigidly on now one, now another of the sheets of paper that are stuffed to overflowing into folders on the desk before her.

Puzzled, I sit for hours, trying to decipher arcane 19th century cursive in a language that I began learning just a few years earlier. Every stroke looks the same. It might as well be the random marks left by a cat in its litter box that I am studying.

I am cold, because the room is frigid, though the secretary, the sentinel of this temple, seems completely impervious to the chilly temperature. I shiver and curse myself for having foolishly abandoned my coat to the rack at the entrance to the building.

I am hungry, because I have not broken the night's fast, wanting to avoid wasting time in the morning so as to get to the shrine at the moment its doors creaked open, as it is locked to the public for all but three hours each day and I need to maximize my time.

I am tired, because I was up late working, every fifteen minutes or so thinking in horror of the price I would pay in the morning for my failure to get to sleep instead of sitting still longer in front of the computer screen.

As my suffering body slumps on the hard, inconceivably and impossibly hard, inhumanly, monstrously, satanically hard chair, I cannot imagine how I will accomplish anything at all. But I sit here anyway, and I chastise myself to continue, and I try to force the fear to back down first.

The clock ticks.

Time hates me and it does not care about my work. At all. It wants only to pass, and to push me out the door, and to hasten the end of days and weeks and months until my time to do this work is gone and I must return with nothing to show for all these cold, hungry, desperately tired mornings sitting in a room with hostile, mockingly and illegibly scribbled sheets of paper and a haughtily indifferent companion who, for all I can tell, may not even know that I am there.

Finally, with utter predictability, the icy premonition of my failure arrives and speaks to me. "*You will not accomplish what you are here to do,*" it announces in a sneering tone. "*You will sit here for hours over many days, and you will be unable to decipher the codes that parade before you and you will struggle futilely against sleep, and you will wish yourself dead a hundred thousand times and eventually you will have to go home, and you will not have done what you set out to do. You will fail.*"

~

Another day, another building.

The sun streams in through high arched windows on the roof of the converted chapel that holds me in its bosom. I am far from the city, in a pristine village that everywhere reminds of its link to history. Saints have been removed from the walls, but their essence has bled into the building itself, and I feel their presence, hear their voices, am guided by their will.

I am a monk, an ascetic withdrawn from the mundane world, listening to the wind in the recesses of the cavernous abbey.

The files arrive, and they are in good order. I scan the pages. The hand is crisp and clear. I fall to the reading with the gusto of a hungry man served a heaping, steaming plate. My mind is untroubled, limpid, my consciousness fully focused on the task. Nothing interferes, nothing distracts. Fatigue does not exist, hunger does not exist, bodily functions have altogether gone on hiatus while I am in the presence of the blessed, mystical documents.

As I devour these holy texts and scribble my notes, a warmth comes over me, despite the icy air outside and the expanse of the old structure in which I sit.

It will all fall into place.

I will make it through all the things I have decided to see here, and they will serve me in the way intended. My planning is vindicated.

The world is dictated by predictability and beauty.

Stepping outside after purchasing an espresso from the vending machine that is fortifying and delicious, far better than should be possible under such circumstances, I walk in the courtyard, and I look to the cloudless sky, my eye reflecting the glint from a crystalline pond.

THE PET RABBIT

MY SISTERS AND I HAD a pet rabbit for a few weeks when we were young. Our mother, who was recognized in our family as the one with the prerogative to name pets, had christened him Pedro.

He was a youngster, so small that he could easily fit into the two hands of a child, friendly and cuddly. I do not remember where we got him. We were very fond of him, and we relished the fact that he was ours to care for and to maintain.

One lovely summer day, a Sunday, we killed him.

It was unintentional, but it was unmistakably our action that took his life. Nothing could be more certain.

That morning, we had left for our grandparents' house, an hour and a half away, for the day. We all bade him farewell. None of the three of us remembered to give him water. It was exceptionally hot, and his pen was on our back porch, which heated up well beyond the external temperature on sunny summer days.

When we returned from Grandma and Grandpa's house, we were all quite cheerful, still buzzing with the energy of the trip. We ran to Pedro's pen to play with him.

He was on his side, shuddering, gasping for air.

In that terrible instant of realization that is the space between happiness and despair, we understood that something was horribly wrong. My mother ascertained the nature of the problem quickly. She got an eyedropper and gave him water. For long minutes, we stood there beside her, hushed in fear and guilt, watching, terrified but not yet completely without hope.

In such moments, when the possibility of two endings presents itself, one heart-rending and the other miraculous, you try to imagine only the miracle. *"Please,"* you plead, *"please, God, may it come to pass. May he be spared and may I be given another chance to show my compassion. Please. Please."* It is too much to think the worst can be true until there are no other options.

It was too late.

He perished in her hands, the three of us gathered around her, praying desperately that she could work a miracle, and then in utter anguish when the miracle did not come.

And then, our hope extinguished, it began to sink in that we alone were responsible for his suffering and his demise. We had been the agents of the agonizing death by dehydration of this being that we so loved. We did it. We alone. We were the authors of his agony.

It was intolerable. We cried inconsolably at the perishing of this little being, shivering so pathetically, so tiny and so helpless. We had wanted only to love him, and he depended on our love to sustain him. But we failed him utterly, and he died.

~

The radio was on during this awful spectacle. One song I can distinctly recall was playing in the background just as all this was reaching its intolerable conclusion, as Pedro died and the full dreadful finality of that and of my responsibility for his end was dawning on me. The song's lyrics tell a tender love story, but it is now forever a song of death and loss for me. I will not name it because to utter its title instantly resurrects the chorus in my brain, and this causes the anguish of that moment to explode back into my consciousness, instantly, devastatingly.

To this day, five decades on, I am overcome with a deep sense of dread whenever I hear or even think of that song, a feeling of darkness and tragedy that will permit no alleviation. It is tingling faintly as I write this. The finality of the grave is the sole, complete meaning of that music for me. When I hear it, even without hearing it when it manifests inside my head against my will, I am again guilty of the most heinous crime: *The lethal failure to give care to a being I claimed to love.*

At my mother's command, I buried him in the back yard. When the somber act was finished, I placed a flat stone over his grave and knelt at the tiny tomb for what seemed an eternity, hearing the sounds of the world around me and yet not hearing them, existing in some space just alongside and separate from my previous life, allowing my emotional haze and confusion to magnify to the point that for an instant I thought it possible I might be dreaming it all, and I hoped with all my desperate child's heart that I might awake and find that the unreality of what was occurring would be in a lightning stroke clarified and undone as I stepped out of the choking mist of the nightmare.

I begged God through scalding tears to make him wake. But there was no awakening, and no alleviation of the unbearable culpability, and no reversal of the tragedy. The rabbit remained dead, below my feet in the ground, and I stood there, a mere boy, exposed to the judgment of a pitiless world.

~

In my endless desire to find unsuspected meaning everywhere, I now see how the name my mother gave this creature should be understood.

Pedro is Peter in Spanish. My mother knows no Spanish beyond the few words every American knows, yet this is the name that came to her. That tongue, a mystery to me at that early point in my life, and a woman who spoke it as her own and who would one day become my wife waited in my future to shape my life and my dreams.

And Peter was the fisherman called to be a fisher of men, the truest of the disciples, who was so vigilant in protection of what he held dearest that he wielded a sword to prevent evil coming to it. The perfect inverse mirror of my failure in such care as a boy, but a model to which to aspire as I left childhood. And Peter was the rock on which was built an edifice of love that has lasted through the millennia and that sheltered me in my later wandering, as, in a place far from Pedro's grave, across an ocean, I sat weeping not in mourning but joyfully in stone churches built by men dead eight hundred years ago.

All of it was there already as a seed, in the name and fate of a little rabbit, and watered by the disconsolate tears of children who loved him.

MEXICAN JUMPING BEANS

ON DECEMBER 21, 2020, I picked up my copy of Roger Caillois' *L'homme et le sacré*, for the first time in a decade.

I found it randomly, looking about for another book, unaware even that the Caillois was there where I found it. It should have been on another shelf, on the other side of the room, according to the logic of my less than perfect home library organizing system.

As the title indicates (*Man and the Sacred*, if we steal away the magic of the French), sacredness is the topic of the Caillois book. I found my copy in a Paris used bookstore, a few minutes' walk from the apartment in which I was then staying near Place Monge. I read a quarter of the book standing right there in the shop next to the shelf from which I had plucked it, mesmerized. In my mind's eye, I can still see every contour of the place, including the winding and claustrophobic staircase that led down to the basement stacks where I discovered the book and the splendid view out the front window of the Rue des Écoles.

Caillois died on December 21, 1978, at the age of just 65. I found his book for the second time, in the labyrinth of my library, on the day of his death, 42 years later.

He and his friend André Breton once had a bitter disagreement about the Mexican jumping bean. What, they wondered, to do about the mystery of the source of the bean's vitality?

Breton argued for accepting the mystery. We do not know, we do not need to know, our joy at the bean's inexplicable motion is not made one iota less euphoric by accepting our ignorance. Indeed, our excitement may depend on it.

Caillois defended the imperative of cutting the bean open to see what engine was driving it, even if this meant the magic of the bean must cease.

More numerology. Breton died the year I was born, on the day that marked the end of my first five months in the world. Thirty years later, on that same day, and without previous knowledge that it was the day of his death, I visited his grave in Paris and took a photo that shows my shadow on his tomb.

Whose side am I on?

I can recall holding a Mexican jumping bean at some distant point in my childhood, purchased at some roadside establishment somewhere off the highway during a family drive to a distant place. I was fascinated. I was also too young then even to recognize the existence of the two conflicting views.

I have however spent the whole of my life since the age of reason pondering the two ways of knowledge and faith, choosing first one, then the other, then reversing, and again, back and forth, indecisive, compelled now by one and now by the other, seeing truth in both and in neither and in only one at a time.

And now, all these years later, whose side am I on?

Perhaps a choice is not necessary.

May one align with Caillois' reasoned inquiry into sacredness, but because of a Bretonian method that is based on the irrational mystery of having stumbled on his book on the day of his death?

I believe I will keep them both with me for the rest of my journey.

THAT MAGICAL SPACE

IF I COULD, I WOULD go back right now, though it was a time full of anxiety, even terror. If I could, I would stay there forever, with all that trepidation and uncertainty, to sense again the vital spark in its first awakening inside me. Roughly 1978 through 1981. In those three years, in that magical space.

I was twelve in 1978. I still can feel my face burning when I recall the embarrassment I felt then at the thought that the girls I knew in school might somehow discern how I had started, inexplicably, to imagine how they looked underneath their clothing as we sat in class a few desks apart and learned algebra.

At around this time, I saw Debbie Harry in the video for Blondie's "Heart of Glass." I was at this age only just beginning to learn that there were substances—some drunk, others smoked—that could "make you high," which meant, in my perspective, that they caused you to look sleepy, with moist and perhaps red eyes, and if you were female, they gave you an aura that was all the more sexually enticing. Debbie Harry's eyes were the eyes of someone who was high, to my twelve-year-old mind.

I was riveted.

⁓

I was an avid reader of science-fiction then. All of the Dune books, a good deal of Arthur C. Clarke, some less notable writers and books too.

But the sci-fi is not what struck me in *Alien*. It was the two points in Sigourney Weaver's t-shirt in the final scenes of the film. The entire plot of the film melted into inconsequentiality when they made their appearance and seared their image into my neurons. My mother and sisters were in the room, watching the movie with me, and I felt certain they could tell just how fervently I watched those disappointingly fleeting scenes and how desperately they affected me.

~

Every Friday night, *The Dukes of Hazzard*. Daisy Duke, with her country girl curves, skimpy shirts, and jean cut-offs. I waited every Friday night, half-following the story of the Duke boys engaging in this or that illegal act and the sheriff chasing them, and then other distracting things happening, while my obsessed attention impatiently waited only for Daisy to come strutting into the room in those shorts and a t-shirt, with a huge smile on her face and a twinkle in her eye.

~

Before MTV, there was a program called Video Concert Hall. Gary Numan's "Cars," some song by Nazareth that featured a kid playing video games although the song had nothing to do with playing video games, a song by a band called Split Enz with a chorus that came mysteriously into my consciousness forty years later one day riding a bike.

One song I saw on this program burrowed into my consciousness like no other. "Garbageman" by a band unfamiliar to me then, the Cramps. Rockabilly punk, and a video shot in a graveyard, apparently, with the lead singer prancing around like a weird ghoul, long fingernails that he pointed around in a menacing way.

I was not much interested in the song itself, though I found the campy horror movie atmosphere of the video to my liking. But one of the two guitar players in the band was female, with frizzy red hair, a leather jacket, and skintight yellow hotpants. She strutted and snarled in such a way that my youthful belly got all warm as I watched her lean against a graveyard monument and ferally rub her back on it and crouch low with her legs splayed, the singer on his back reverently gazing up her thighs at the point where they joined as she strummed that guitar. Lip curled, tights clinging to her legs and her sex, eyes darkly made up and distant, inviting and unapproachable at once, impossibly, overwhelmingly erotic.

I will see her like that for the rest of my life, even should she die before me. I see her there now, though she is an old woman. Eternal woman sex power. A vision of rock 'n' roll bad girl unattainability for the boy even then being remade by hormonal revolutions into something else, something else entirely.

Only later, I discovered the singer in the band, who was her lover, was just like me, nothing more fancy or sophisticated than a fucked-up loser kid from Ohio. If I had known this when I was lusting after Poison Ivy, it would have driven me mad, because it would have seemed possible that I too could have a girl like that. Much later, I learned the name of the album that contained this song was the brilliantly transgressive "Songs the Lord Taught Us."

The singer, Lux Interior, has since died. Perhaps he is somewhere, floating, insubstantial, unseen, remembering wistfully that girl with the frizzy hair and the guitar in her yellow hotpants and leather jacket, thinking of the times he touched those thighs, mourning that he can never do so again, in glorious tears reliving the experiences of the flesh in ghostly wisps of undying will and desire.

〜

"Tempted." A pristinely sad chorus about a love lost because of infidelity, with a smooth descending bass line. And a dancing New Wave blonde, in a thin shirt with no bra, a blue skirt with a red belt, her eyes heavily mascaraed, her hair jaggedly cut, her expression lit up with an imperiously gorgeous punk girl smile, a perfect Roman line of a nose and ruby red lipstick, her hips angularly twitching and twisting, in the awkwardly, peculiarly sexy way I imagined only British punk rockers could manage. Oh, tempted, indeed. I find the song forty years later on YouTube, and the comments section reveals I was not the only one with a crush on her.

⌒

This same year, Stevie Nicks cut "Stop Draggin' My Heart Around" with Tom Petty, and in the video, toward the end of the song, she finished her verse and turned to watch Petty start his, looking at him out of the corner of her eye, in the background of the shot, with an expectant gaze. Not smiling but presaging something beyond smiles. The look every beautiful woman flashes when she knows she is beautiful and she knows you are looking at her and thinking how beautiful she is and knowing she is beyond your reach, and she knows it too but just wants to look at you with that look that says just how wonderful it would be if only she would look at you with longing. Her look is decidedly not that look of longing, but a look that causes the one who sees it to want that face to wear the emotion of longing more desperately than anyone has wanted anything since the beginning of the entire world.

I was fifteen years old seeing her face.

⌒

"Words." I liked the song, even though it should have been too New Agey for my tastes at the time. A heavy guitar sound, a drummer who I later learned had played a long stint in Zappa's band, a badge of honor indicating superior chops in the rock world, and a minimalist aesthetic, the stage area draped in white paper, and the musicians all dressed in black. But the song was not the point. The singer, Dale Bozzio, the drummer's wife, as it turned out, and a former Playboy model, stands basically nude, a tape recorder strapped over her pubic area, her hair platinum blonde with a shock of blue and pink on one side, two small metallic-looking panels over her breasts, standing mostly stock still on her two long naked legs, her upper body rocking to and fro seemingly unattached to her lower half. Eroticism of a kind so raw my fifteen-year-old brain and body were fairly singed by the atomic blast. The movement of those breasts and those hips, all the universe itself contained in that motion.

AN ODD COUPLE
AND THEIR CITY

BY PURE CHANCE, Charles Baudelaire and Diana, Princess of Wales, died on the same date, one hundred and thirty years apart.

In the early morning hours of August 31, 1997, Diana's life ended in a destroyed automobile that had just run at high speed into a concrete pillar in a tunnel beneath the Pont de l'Alma in Paris.

I was at the time sleeping in my tiny sublet apartment near Place d'Italie, about three miles away from the crash site. As her body was lying in the hospital where she was declared dead, I was getting into the taxi that would take me to Charles de Gaulle airport for my flight back to the US after a lengthy stay in the City of Light. It was on the taxi's radio that I heard the news.

In the bag that I would carry on to the plane that morning was a paperback copy of Baudelaire's *Le Spleen de Paris*, which I had been reading and rereading in the weeks since I bought it for a few francs in one or another of the Paris bookstores that I had haunted during my stay.

I can recall watching part of Diana's wedding to then-Prince Charles in 1981. It was in the early hours here in the US. The month was late July, so I was not in school, but would have been up early to deliver the morning paper that was my source of income for a few years as a teen. Like everyone else here in the US, I had heard a good deal about the wedding, and I certainly knew how precisely the 19-year-old bride-to-be fit the mythical parameters of The Princess. I thought at the time that she looked something like an older sister of a girl I knew and who was the first object of my then just emerging romantic interest.

The Pont de l'Alma was finished about a decade before Charles Baudelaire's death on the last day of August in 1867, so it is possible he might have walked upon it. The earthquake of a book of poetry for which he is known by every schoolchild in France, even now in the age of encroaching multiculturalist education there, *Les Fleurs du mal*, was published about a year after the bridge was built.

I had crossed the Pont de l'Alma, though only a few times, as it was distant, at least on foot, from the neighborhoods I frequented in the hearts of the 5th and 6th arrondissements. Two other bridges over the Seine near the Alma, the Pont Alexandre III and the Pont d'Iena, the latter of which abuts the Eiffel Tower on one side of the river and the lovely Trocadéro Gardens and Esplanade on the other, were more frequent walkways for me during my divagations around the city.

Far and away, the Paris bridge of my greatest affection remains the Pont Mirabeau, not only because of Apollinaire's poem but because it was the bridge over which I walked dozens of times in 2013 and 2014 while on sabbatical leave, as I made the trip back from my oldest daughter's school on rue du Théâtre in the 15th to our apartment not far from the Stade Roland Garros in the 16th.

Diana and this other Charles, two people who lived and became myths and then died too early and now live on as still more magically powerful myths in the heads of many of us still alive. An odd couple, linked only by the date and the city of their demise, though I suspect Baudelaire might have dedicated at least a few lines to her had he been around in July 1981. But if he had been here then, we would not know of him, as the space that mythologized him and that which mythologized her are separated by an infinite cultural distance.

I am pleased beyond reasonable measure to find this thread to connect them and to send a few words to the heavens on their day in praise of both myths: *Pristine beauty and storybook love, sparkling and tormented artistic genius.* Live forever, beautiful emblems of human glory!

TEN MILES ALONG THE
PERIPATETIC WAY

I WENT FOR A WALK ONE DAY. Started in Hummels Wharf, and ended at home in Lewisburg, about ten or eleven miles. An even ten, for aesthetic purposes.

Walking and thought are intimately bound up together. Or once were. I once, long ago, tried to hold peripatetic office hours during which students who wanted to consult with me would be apprised of the map of a perambulatory circuit I made around campus at the assigned hour so they could accurately predict where I was likely to be at any given time and come join me for a walking chat. Nobody came. A shattering failure. I had then not yet come to fully understand how far our world is from the world that once was in which people walked and thought as a matter of course.

Walking long distances—anything more than a half hour or so counts—inevitably leads me to new places, not just in the geographical but also in the mental sense. I should do it more, I tell myself constantly, but I find an infinite number of reasons not to do so, diseased as I am by our times and the foolishness to which I often give in.

One of the many productive things on which you can meditate while walking is to stop assaulting yourself for not doing all the things you should do more often and to just be happy for this one time that you did not find a reason to avoid doing the desirable thing.

⌒

I walked railroad tracks a lot when I was a boy.

Not on them, mind you, but alongside and at a safe distance. Even young, I had a sense of what kind of destruction a train can wreak on a human being, probably because of the horror fiction I read so much of in those days. Although I never walked around with things inserted in my ears as kids do today, I knew how easily I got lost in thought and how that translated into decreased acoustic vigilance.

Like many another adolescent, I had youthful dreams of a nomadic existence, but I never fantasized about the actual life of the guys who rode trains and lived as transients, as I had met a few of them and knew a little of how dismally hard and short that life is. I saw two fighting with knives once on the tracks from a bridge safely overhead. That alone would have cured any mythologies about that state of existence.

But I did sometimes wonder what it would be like to walk many miles every day, lost internally, pondering deep questions, never speaking to anyone, just looking at the world pass by and feeling my legs drive me forward, reflecting on the wind and the sun and the trees and sundry other matters. I thought sometimes I would live in the woods one day as Thoreau had, bears and mountain lions my neighbors, but as a youth I was still too attracted to the affairs of cities to practically pursue this.

Walking simplifies. It clears out clutter, and human life—my life— is cluttered.

You get a more concrete idea of just how much clutter there is in the human world when you walk roadside. Beer cans, every conceivable part of a car, mud-caked clothing, discarded boxes and bottles, cigarette butts and packages, decomposing fast food and the containers in which it was served, rope, twine, tools, pieces of carpet, floor mats, utterly unidentifiable trash, objects of which I am ignorant of name and purpose.

I saw a couple of stuffed animals that had clearly been there for weeks or months, aesthetically weathered in such a way as to sorrowfully communicate the fallenness of a world in which a child's beloved stuffed bear, with which she cuddled nightly to ward off the darkness, could be so callously abandoned to the cruelties of the elements. I saw them in a midday sun-drenched area that I was trying in my short sleeves to get through quickly and back into the cool of shade, so I did not take the time to stop and take what I imagine would have been a poignant photo that now can only be imagined.

I saw a shoe and then, a half mile further along, its mate. What is their story?

We put all of it beside the road when we are done with it, sometimes stopping to do so, sometimes just slowing down and indifferently flipping it out the window and then going on our way, forgetting what we tossed altogether in minutes as fresh stimuli collide with our senses. Transience is at the roadside like weeds and the smell of gasoline. Almost none of our stuff persists. We pursue it ferociously, and we get it, and then in short order we tire of it and discard it.

Imagine two people who work for a company that makes some consumer product or other. One invents a means to make the product last ten times longer for no increased production cost. The other comes up with a way to ensure that a vital part of the product will self-destruct after a short and highly predictable period of time, and it will do so in a way that corrupts the entire device so the single part cannot simply be replaced but a whole new product must be purchased. Which employee is given a promotion and which is let go in contemporary America?

Our lives are a long drive through a huge mountain range of objects we kept around for a while and then tossed aside. At some point, the whole planet will appear as a vast, endless hoarder's apartment, every inch of space stacked ten feet high with somebody's things they absolutely had to have but then they did not.

∽

As I walked, I meditated on the idea of the impermanence of the self.

There is no coherent, enduring, categorically stable "I" because everything that makes up my body, including my brain, is constantly in flux, and these material objects are, it is assumed, the only things we could mean when we say "I," and any subjective experience we identify with self is dependent on them for existence. Cells are dying and new ones are being born every second. Synaptic connections fall into disuse and decay while new experiences create novel such connections. This is true at every point along the time trajectory, so by this approach the I (or what I mistakenly take to be "I") that photographed the shoe disintegrated into nothingness the instant it finished that action and took a step away from the shoe, further down the road. And the same as I took the second step. Many, many people were on my ten-mile walk, together in a sense, yet in succession, and each one alone.

Heraclitus's "You never step in the same stream twice"—or the embellishment of "You can never step into the same stream even once"—is true in a purely material sense. There can be no doubt about this. It is different molecules of water each time, and even during the one step. But I contend that for all intents and purposes I am the same me that began and ended the walk, even in the materialist terms of the argument. Enough of the baseline remained intact to make the fiction a meaningful and constructive one. If I had been struck by a vehicle and hit my head hard enough to scramble it but not hard enough to perish, then it is surely a different "I." But there is sufficient continuity in my case that I remember thoughts I had in high school like I had them yesterday, and they are pristinely consistent with everything I know to be me, though they passed through a brain that featured a collection of neurons that is not the brain and collection of neurons with which I write these words. (Neurons, it turns out, are regenerated even in adulthood.)

And there is something else to it.

I have in times past been quite sympathetic to reductive materialism. Some of the arguments are elegant, and the scientifically validated evidence is cleanly on this side. But there exist other kinds of evidence. How does it come to pass that a mere meat puppet cannot accept the inevitability of going the way of meat and instead desires, fervently, with all its energy and all its heart, to live forever?

～

There is roadkill at the roadside as well.

All the living things that we turn into non-living things with our giant fast-moving metal transport machines. Have you ever thought about the magnitude of this feature of the roadway? It is breathtaking. Precise numbers are made hard to approximate because of technical problems and our lack of interest, but the figure is certainly in the many billions globally per year. In Brazil alone, half a billion animals are killed by cars annually. That is a five with eight zeros after it. Sixty-five thousand deer are killed on roadways every year in New York State alone.

"Roadkill" is actually a dreadfully industrial-sounding term, and technically quite incorrect. After all, the road did not kill these once living creatures. The people who made the decision to get into the vehicles that they then propelled into and through their bodies did it. Distancing from moral responsibility is everywhere in language. We like to try to hide from the havoc we wreak on the world.

I once drove in a friend's car through the desolate Nevada desert north of Winnemucca at night on US 95. We were far from any hotel, hungry, desperate to get somewhere that was not the desert. My memory of it is that we hit a jackrabbit crossing the road every minute or so. Every sixty seconds, and sometimes still more frequently, for more than an hour before we left the desert. They were unavoidable, given the darkness and the proximity of deep brush to the edge of the two-lane road on which we were driving. We felt sick about it.

But we kept driving.

Jains, when waking at night to change sleeping positions, sweep the floor before lying down in a new place in order to avoid potentially crushing an insect in doing so. It is an impossible task they have taken up—their immune systems are, like ours, constantly carrying out a ruthless holocaust of micro-organisms, and there is nothing any of us can do about that—but still I find something deeply admirable about them. They take the problem seriously. How many of us even slow down to avoid hitting the squirrel that bolts in front of us on an apparent suicide mission?

I was particularly moved by a dead snake, now mostly skeleton. Called by the heat of the asphalt, or seeking prey or escape from a predator, its journey in the world ended here at the roadside. I took a picture of it with my phone, and now I have preserved it for a period of time in the world of pixels, in my computer's hard drive, that will almost certainly exceed the time it spent in scale and bone. A leaf in the photo just next to the snake's remains bears witness until it too disintegrates and is no more.

I felt like I was doing what I could to repent for the sin some anonymous member of my species committed in destroying this marvelous creature whose kind have been here for one hundred fifty million years, who were gliding across the earth long before even our earliest primate ancestors existed.

~

It is an uncanny feeling being on foot beside a busy road.

I always walk on the left side, as far from the road as possible, so I can see the traffic approaching. This is mostly to do with my total lack of trust that motorists at my back will have anything like the concern for my life that I have. This seems a reasonable estimation. I care more about me than they do, certainly, and I want to have at least a split second to leap out of the way of negligent drivers if need be.

When you walk against the traffic, for a few seconds you can see the faces of all those fellow humans zooming off to their destinations. The constant stream of humanity in their gleaming painted boxes. A never-ending supply. At no hour of the day does it stop completely, and even when it is a mere trickle in one place, it is a torrent in many others.

We have achieved the nomadism of which I dreamt as a boy! But not quite. Always on the go and always seeking to go farther and yet farther and farther still, and at greater and greater speeds, and with less and less connection to what we pass over during the journeys. Where is home in such a life?

⌒

For some, home is where the pigs are.

About three miles in physical distance from the Bucknell University campus where I work, minutes in a car, light years in cultural terms, is a house that I have driven past hundreds of times. Yet before this walk I had never realized there were two grown pigs living in a pen in the front yard. The guy next door came over when I waved to him and we had a nice chat about the state of the world, cars, and pigs.

He said the pigs have names. Something like Lola and Lonnie, if my recollection is good.

⌒

Another house I passed presented a haunting image. Its stone staircase was utterly dissolved by the years, making the home unreachable by its entryway. The house was right next to an old church. I tried the front entrance of the latter, but it was locked. I would have liked to sit down in a cool spot to ponder the symbolism of that ravaged staircase.

I was starting to get thirsty, having foolishly failed to bring adequate water. A receptionist in an auto repair shop with a tattoo completely covering one arm and shoulder let me use the faucet there. She saved me a headache, if not something worse. I have had near heat strokes a few times in my life, once after playing too much basketball outside in the summer southern California sun, again while moving furniture from a storage space on a blazing August day in central Pennsylvania. Those experiences are to my mind an approximation of what might await the unrepentant in Hell.

This was the first time in a long while that I had taken up a walk of this distance, and I was pleasantly surprised at how little protest my aging body mounted. Other than thirst, not a twinge of resistance from the machine I inhabit. I rested for ten minutes two or three times, and I stopped more frequently for briefer periods of time to take several dozen pictures.

Even when such physical exertion goes well, I try to keep one thing firmly in mind: *The time will come, sooner than you desire even if it is delayed to its maximum possibility, when you will no longer be able to do this. There will thus be a last time. Think of this one as the last.*

The aging of the body is on my mind frequently these days. I find it an odd and disconcerting thing indeed to discover myself in a human form that looks as this one does, that is, clearly no longer young. Is it correct that we all form a mind's eye view of ourselves that never alters with age, even as our physical reality moves to greater and greater distance from that image? I do not know if it is a general phenomenon, but I certainly have done this. The self-image inside my head is from about twenty-five years in the past now. I never much enjoyed looking at myself in a mirror. I actively avoid it now, so jarring is it for me to see the reality of time's work.

I hope to get better at this, as nothing good comes from this failure to face reality. I am not sure what the process of that improvement might look like, though. It is a harrowing aspect of aging. But then, are there any that are not harrowing when properly considered?

The house with the staircase crumbled to rubble. By the ceaseless advance of time.

～

Hidden from sight from the road, or at least only available to a fleeting glimpse at fifty miles per hour insufficient to the beauty of the site, I found an idyllic stream accented with delicately shaped outcroppings of rock and a stone bridge peeking through dense foliage.

Beauty is almost always like this. Fail to look in the right place and you miss it. Stop paying attention for an instant and it is gone. Drink your fill of it while you can, in the instants you find yourself before it, because soon you must move on and there is no certainty it will be there the next time you pass by. Wait long enough and the certainty is that it will not.

～

After a journey of several hours, I was greeted by a vision as I was nearing home. As I stopped in a field of six-inch high wild grass and other vegetation, including an ocean of familiar flowering weeds with stalks reaching up determinedly toward the sky, I looked westward to a line of trees at the top of the hill. The descending sun was gently glowing at the borders of the trees and creating a play of colors there and in the verdant field that nearly took my breath away.

I had settled in my mind an important matter I was considering just a few minutes before, and the sun decided to be just where it was, and those trees had been waiting their whole lives to reach just this height and breadth and to glow in the sun's light in just this way, and these delightful weeds (ribwort plantain, *Plantago lanceolata*, I discover), which I have seen all my life without knowing a proper name to give them, stretched up longingly from the grass, a sea of little sentinels awaiting my passage, standing at attention for the portrait I took of them.

The walk is now but a trace of life past. It came and went, like everything else. I wish I could have kept it with me in some way, but that is not possible. Even to do it again tomorrow will not do the trick. It would be a new walk.

What I do here, with words, is the doomed attempt to keep it.

SUFFERING AND HOPE

THE SOUND OF YOUR TWO VOICES is a café and a used bookstore, drifting through the streets of Hillcrest, North Park, University Heights, Normal Heights, Kensington in the last decade of the last century. It is the sun on my face and my feet on the sidewalk as I make my pilgrimage daily, stopping at every altar to drink, eat, read, wonder what my life will be in that sacrosanct time yet to come.

At each holy shrine, I find a table, set a pile of books before me, pull out a notebook and pen, prepare for the rite.

At each altar, I hear you, sometimes through speakers, sometimes resonating in my memory.

~

Lilting, effervescent, eternally youthful, that smile wise beyond your years, that lovely brogue that would melodically melt stone into pure passion.

Eyes downcast as listeners sit rapt in attention, grasping desperately at every fragile syllable you whisper as though each one held an infinite bounty.

I thought then, in the tunnel vision that afflicts those fresh in this world, that I would hear the both of you forever, not just as I sat in the laundromat on Park Street and thumbed through Hegel, but also when I was old, in that time that then, as always, could not even really be imagined.

I hoped you would never grow old.

～

Dolores, sufferings. Like all of us, you knew pain, abuse, sorrow, and depression. Like many fewer, you also knew joy and success and tremendous wealth and the standing of royalty in the country of your birth. You were gone before you could grow old, carried away in the waters of your bath that January night in London.

You had called your mother in the wee hours, and you were found submerged and cold in the tub later that morning, four times the legal limit of alcohol in your system. The terrible inevitability with which something many of us do and almost all survive nonetheless stills the hearts of a few.

You go to join that choir of joyous voices that brought so much delirious happiness to so many and that were yet haunted by their own sorrows to an early departure from this realm.

～

I went to an open mic poetry night at one of those cafés where they played your music.

The readings were as one expects under such conditions. I started to leave, but I stopped under the force of your sincerity. I sat there and listened to these bad poets, and I tried to imagine the fearful and wonderful things that had happened to them and that served as the impetus for the words they used so imperfectly to try to communicate their hurt and their joy and their vulnerability and their overcoming and their gratitude.

I forgave them for their inability to bring the thing they were trying to express to life and embraced their honest, naked desire to speak to all of us in the room gathered there, each nursing his own failures and incompleteness.

~

In a dream, Dolores, I leave the café poetry reading and somehow appear in your hotel room, just as you are slipping beneath the water's surface, and I pull you from the water, and you gasp for air for a minute, and you cough a few times, and then you are fine.

And there also with us in the dream—how could it be otherwise with such an ending?—is Hope.

I give you a towel to cover and dry. We do not say a word, the three of us. It does not even occur to me to tell you how much your voices haunt me because I suspect in dreams you would know such things.

Then, still in the dream, we fall, the three of us. It is a soundless, blind falling, and even though we know it cannot end well, we are very happy. We enjoy the breeze that streaks the tears across our faces.

Still falling, as that is our condition, which you knew even in the bloom of youth. But what joy to know that you, Dolores, for a moment, are no longer breathless, and you accompany us.

And Hope, eyes dark and hair electric, is whispering something that I cannot hear but that I nonetheless know to be true.

WHAT THE MONKS
ARE DOING

I AM SEATED IN A 1982 VOLVO, headed north on I-5 toward Oceanside, albeit at a pace I could easily best on a bicycle. The universe of cars spreads out north and south in what appears an infinite expanse. How can people live like this? Twenty-five miles will take an hour or more, on a five-lane freeway. The torturous ordeal of Southern California rush hour traffic can only quite imperfectly be communicated in its soul-deadening wickedness to anyone who has not directly experienced it.

Through the speakers in the car, I hear Alanis Morissette's howling. It is 1995, and "You Oughta Know" has exploded her and her voice into the consciousness of everyone within earshot of an FM radio dial. From the open window, the infernal blare of horns and the acrid stench of exhaust flood in. The crush of humanity is palpable, each of us tucked into our large, barely moving boxes of metal and plastic as we collectively but disappointingly slowly make our way to our destinations. Our technology designed for speed has been defeated utterly by our determined inability to master space and population.

My sense of futility is as heavy as the pollution emanating from the tailpipes of all these vehicles. Why am I even bothering? I will not make it on time. My conscience, my seemingly congenital inability, perhaps due to what is diagnosable OCD, to begin anything in mid-stream because of an overwhelming sense that this intolerably corrupts the aesthetics of the entire affair, makes it impossible to participate in the intended affair at all if I arrive late.

I contemplate turning around and going home. But if I do that, I will have the same unbearable traffic on an overheated highway to endure, and with the added burden of having failed to do what I set out to do. I doggedly keep driving.

And then, there is a break in the wave of cars. I accelerate, exhilarated to be moving at a proper clip again, hoping the reprieve will last long enough to get me to the exit.

It does. Abruptly, I am off the freeway. It is a mile from the exit to the road that will take me where I am going.

Now I am ascending a hill, the breeze in my face.

The road winds and twists, and there are precipitous drops. I proceed cautiously, fearful of the disaster that might be coming toward me around each bend, though I have seen no other cars since I began my ascent.

I round one more curve, and now I have arrived at the top of the hill.

There is an abbey at the summit.

~

The Prince of Peace Abbey still sits on its hill in Oceanside, California, a half hour's distance in the absence of rush hour traffic from the campus of the school where, a quarter century ago, I pursued graduate study. Some two dozen monks live and work and sing and pray there. I was on that day in 1995 coming to hear them celebrate the office of Vespers and to share in their prayer.

This was a tumultuous period in my life. I was finally nearing the end of my time in school and thinking with some trepidation about what I would do next, in my early 30s with an advanced degree but quite limited job prospects. More profoundly, I was in a spiritual crisis. My long period of easy atheism, a product of a youth adrift from religious instruction and a stubborn impatience with authority of any sort, had of late been troubled by personal catastrophes. The most traumatizing of these were the deaths of both of my siblings in foreseeable but still horrific tragedies. Something that had been asleep during the forgetfully distracted years of youth had opened its eyes and it was gnawing away at me internally.

In high school, I had read Bertrand Russell's *Why I am not a Christian* and found it sufficiently convincing that I had immediately, and entirely uncritically, adopted a firm opposition to all religious practice. Russell was a towering intellectual figure, the author of a history of philosophy from which I had read dribs and drabs and been duly impressed. He described Christianity as not only ignorant but directly harmful to human well-being. The decision was made. This would be the way of seeing the world with which I would one day, far in the future, die. I was certain of it.

And then I was brought back to the knife edge of this world by the disappearance, untimely, of those two whom I had loved more than any others. My two sisters, not even four years apart, were torn away, each still in her twenties, in circumstances so dreadful I cannot even tell the stories without returning viscerally and painfully to that loss, and so to save myself another reliving of that agony, I will not tell them.

As I struggled with these events, a friend on campus, someone with whom I shared important childhood experiences and a deep love of some of the same music, told me there was a place north of campus where one could find the quiet needed to hear what one needed to hear in times like this. He drove me there the first time. We did not speak at all in the car on the way, nor at the abbey, nor on the ride home.

But I knew something important had happened.

~

We have no effective calculus for taking the measure of how much the scale of cosmic morality is moved in the direction of good by the work done by monks.

Those at the Prince of Peace, under the Order of Saint Benedict, take a vow of stability. This means they stay in the same place for the remainder of their lives. The life of the monk includes all the work necessary to keep the facility operative. Food must be prepared and served, cleaning and repairs must be done, the grounds must be tended. Daily, the monks rise before the sun comes up and meet for collective silent prayer in the chapel at 5:30 a.m. An hour and a half later, their voices puncture the day's silence with a sung prayer. They perform the full day's schedule of Divine Offices, including Holy Mass in the late morning. "The main purpose of our life," reads an informational page on the Abbey's webpage, "is to pray." One can imagine even their practical work as an element in their prayer, a repeated and loving contribution of their spiritual and physical energy to a good beyond them as individuals.

You can see the Pacific Ocean from the monastery.

Construction on the Abbey began in the late 1950s. By the mid-'60s, the monks there had built it up impressively. One of the founding generation, Brother Benno Garrity, tirelessly baked bread and drove about the community collecting donations to distribute to the poor. He so inspired a local couple, Harold and Kay Kutler, that they established a soup kitchen, which eventually became a source of general services material and immaterial to the poor, and named it after him.

Brother Benno passed in 1991, the same year I came to southern California, and before my first trip to the Abbey, so I never knew him. I am certain though, as certain as I can be of anything in this precarious world, that the prayers he prayed during his time there, and all those other prayers of all the other men who passed their lives there and whose bodies were lain to rest in the cemetery there, contributed in some palpable way to my stumbling upon the Abbey.

Over the years, it has become evident to me that I am indebted to these men. I feel they were an essential link holding me, during a time of turmoil and uncertainty in my life, fast to the sacred. In *Thoughts in Solitude*, Merton reflects on the power of the prayer of those in monastic hermitage. The monk's freedom from the worldly involvement of the rest of his kind enables a concentration of prayer unattainable elsewhere. In monastic solitude, he writes, "[m]y whole life becomes a prayer. My whole silence is full of prayer." The monk's orison is not abstract or motivated solely by self-cultivation through *askesis*. Prayer is necessarily an act of petition for the monk, as he is, Merton writes, "more than anyone else . . . always aware of his poverty and of his needs before God." The monk asks in prayer for God's intervention and his prayer extends directly from his need.

Through his constant concentration and application, the monk comes to understand that his prayer is always efficacious, "always answered." Merton is careful to note, however, that the monk must know that the answers are not his, but God's. Surely, we must know that God's answer to the prayers of such men, dedicated to a selfless life of care for the well-being of all souls, would include spiritual balm for those outside the monasteries struggling with loss and desperate for just such aid.

～

I am at the summit of the hill.

Hurriedly, I park the car and I jog to the cemetery. Here, adjacent to the chapel, on the side of the property overlooking the ocean, lie the monks formerly resident who have concluded their earthly travels. The stations of the cross are next to the holy ground in which their mortal remains were interred. I walk and pray. But my concentration is poor, as by the combination of my own imperfections and the dreadful congestion of the I-5, I have arrived just in time for the beginning of the office of Vespers.

Anger at my inability to focus creeps slowly through my nervous system. I try to calm myself before I enter, but that work is accomplished not by me but by the very air inside the Abbey. As I walk through the doors, the music begins. Organ tones waft through the chapel. The monks are already there, lined up in perfect formation, a heavenly order sent to serve as an example to the rest of our anarchist kind.

A handful of souls sit heads down in the pews. The voices of the brothers break the silence, emerging into our shared world, rising up from some place beneath the ground and beyond the sky. They sing the plainchant, this invaluable gift handed down to us by forefathers who were our betters in every way, given freely to a people so undeserving of it that we do not even begin to fathom just how far above us it hovers. *The human voice.* That we can sing almost makes one wonder that, despite our stupidities and our sinfulness, we might be the reason the universe exists.

At the conclusion of the office, I sit in the pews alone, weeping inconsolably, moved by something in a hymn that has struck me at just the right angle, with just the right force. A monk sees me and comes over to put his arm over my shoulder as I shudder and sob. He does not speak. He just comforts me. I pray silently as his hand rests on my back. "*Lord, listen to my prayer. I stretch out my hand, my soul is a land without water. Help me. Please.*"

The sun bursts through the stained window behind the altar, finding me in my desolation and my misery and my loneliness.

The monks' chants are still reverberating in my ears. The tears are still streaming down my face. The unseen action of the prayers of these men, whose sole purpose in life is to pray for their souls and ours, is working away busily, efficaciously, tirelessly, inevitably outside the bounds of my awareness.

Cardinal Newman, in Robert Payne's account, described the Benedictine monk's attitude as "having neither hope nor fear of anything below; in daily prayer, daily bread, and daily work, one day being just like another, except that it was one step nearer than the day before it to that great Day which would swallow up all days, the day of everlasting rest."

If I should be saved from the fate I deserve and find everlasting rest, perhaps their contribution to this undeserved redemption will have been decisive.

OLD CRABTREE

THIS MAN, OF STOOPED BACK and gnarled fingers, of bald pate and just discernibly trembling hands, I knew him from the earliest I remember. He was always this man. I found it impossible to imagine him as at all different, as young, a boy, or even as a newly married man still unpossessed of the large brood of children he and his wife would produce over several decades. My life began too late in his for me to have any reasonable frame of reference to make real the obvious truth that he was not always the grandfather I knew. He barely changed in appearance from the time of my first memory of him to the last time, even if he had during this time become much frailer. His voice, the aspect of a person that counts the most for us, beyond the shape and contour of his face, remained the same flat, country drawl for all the thirty years we shared in this world.

He was for me not wholly a being of flesh and blood. He was as much myth as man.

My mother's father. A walking symbol of the America that is no more, the nineteenth century rural individualist, though technically born at the end of the first decade of the twentieth century. Sturdy and self-sufficient, he worked a farm and repaired telephone lines, soiled overalls his only attire, all year long. A man who in my mind's eye rose from his bed every morning before the sun pierced the horizon and the rooster's crow announced the conclusion of the night, took his breakfast of biscuits, gravy, and black coffee, and headed off to the barn or to the field to work the day long with his hands.

He was an eccentric man. He often told me of conversations he had with various people I presumed to be his inventions. Fictional men of the woods whom he would encounter while out wandering in the wilderness and who would pass along to him fascinating little stories or glowing tidbits of wisdom that my grandfather then duly related to us after dinner.

The chief of these mythological figures was Old Crabtree. From early in my childhood, I remember tales of Old Crabtree and sayings of Old Crabtree and the presence of Old Crabtree through his invocation.

"*I saw Old Crabtree today, he said it looks like rain tomorrow.*"

"*Old Crabtree must have done that.*"

"*Wonder what Old Crabtree'd say about that?*"

Old Crabtree often accomplished amazing feats. He once pulled a broken-down car, single-handed, all the way from town back to the farm. He could speak to and be understood by bears and other wild animals. He routinely climbed to the tops of telephone poles and tall trees for no other reason than to see what could be seen from such a vantage point and to shout that news to anyone within hearing.

I never met Old Crabtree. My grandmother once answered my question about him with something to the effect of "*Oh, Grandpa is just telling tall tales.*" I came to accept Old Crabtree as part of Grandpa's spirited eccentricity, much like the conversations he had with the hogs he raised. Old Crabtree was Grandpa's version of Pecos Bill or Paul Bunyan.

Only later did I come to my present theory about the origins of Old Crabtree. The sometimes comedic, sometimes astounding, always inspiring adventures of Old Crabtree were a mechanism for brightening a world that could be very hard indeed. The life of my grandfather was an ordeal. He worked hard all of the many decades he was given and had little to show for it at the end. He and his wife of seventy-five years had eight children, three of whom died young, two as babies. The third was spirited away from this realm at age thirteen after a life of painful anguish. This last, just older than my mother, was a girl I never knew, who died well before I was born. I have a yellowing photo of her, angelic smile, twinkling eyes, full of joy only a few years from her death. She comes to me in my dreams to assure me that she did live and she did die and we are one flesh, she and I.

My grandfather passed away at the age of ninety-four. I was one of those asked to address the other mourners, mostly my family, at his gravesite, the first time I had ever done such a thing.

I believe it was the first time I had thought hard about the imposing task of speaking of someone you loved at his funeral. We dare to discourse on the recently dead as they repose in their coffins and prepare to be lowered into the earth, to sum up their lives, relationships, meanings in a sprinkling of words under the sun on a country hillside, words offered up in a fleeting few minutes to the breeze and the trees and wild spaces, soon forgotten, perhaps never even heard in the midst of thoughts and tears.

How could I speak of this man, of the time we had together? Of the place he would hold in my memory and in my person and in my soul until my own destruction? Of my love for him and of my bitter understanding that I would never hear his voice again or watch his old eyes sparkle with mischief or feel his hand on my shoulder or hear him relate any further deeds of the legendary Old Crabtree?

Any words, all words fail before this, and mine too failed.

As we laid him to rest up on a hill a few miles from where he had lived nearly his whole life, and I wished that I could make someone know what I felt about him, my eye fell on the tombstone adjacent to the plot where he would lie.

It read—and I swear this is not a tall tale—"Crabtree" with dates of birth and death.

I could almost hear Grandpa laughing somewhere.

THE HARP, THE VOID,
THE PROMISE

DEVISED IMPROVISATIONALLY WITH A PIANO in just intonation, and named for a mythical harp abandoned by European sailors and left to the weather to be played by the marine winds on the California coast, these haunting melodies confront the listener with the stark solitude of that imagined cliff on which, in the legend, Drake's men abandoned the engine that produced them.

In hearing the first ghostly chords and melodies of this work, Terry Riley's *The Harp of New Albion*, I invariably begin a meditation on how alone we are. At first, it is unsettling and frightening. How unfamiliar the relationships between the tones, how evocative of estrangement and distance. They remind me of that abandonment of the instrument that made those sounds. They embody it in their own strange nature.

Those notes take on the shape of my own solitude and of the loneliness that seems deeply rooted in our nature. They come to speak of something empty at the heart of the human condition. How separated we are from one another, constitutionally, by definition, in the very core of what constitutes our inner life. How complete that separation is. How total is our inability to bridge the gap between the self and the other.

And, for this reason, how awfully mine and mine alone must be the unthinkable catastrophe of my death. None can share it. None but I can know it. None can take away its awful power and terror. None can aid or comfort me in the slightest way. No science, no technologies, no politics, none of that in which we place so much desperate hope in this world can prevent it coming to make of my life a ruin and a wreck and a failure and a non-existence and an emptiness and a nothingness and a void and a forever never again and a disappearance into silence that cannot even be said to go on for all time but that is the silence that sits vast and awesome and all incomprehensible outside the boundary of time.

Into that, we are all hurtling, at a speed that is ever increasing, and everything leads us there. Our pleasures and our miseries, our joys and our pains, our contentment, our anxiety, our moments well lived, our hours and days and weeks and years wasted and never to be retrieved.

We are finite. We come and we go. We do not endure. We are a flickering pale flame, barely giving off enough light by which to see these words on a screen, or on a page, for a few seconds, before the darkness reemerges and swallows the photons of light into its boundless belly.

What is it to accept the truth?

To accept the truth is to know, in your gut, with the same dread certainty that you understand that placing your hand into the fire will cause pain and injury, that the day will come when you will no longer be.

To look carefully, steadily, meditatively, at the complete and utter annihilation of your body, your brain, the mass of matter sitting inside your skull that somehow made everything you are, to know that all of that will be the food and then the waste of beetles and worms and bacteria in the soil, and then scattered flotsam and jetsam of the air and mire, blown about by the breeze as the merest dust.

To know too that this dreadful shipwreck will come to your children, and to their children, and to their children's children, to all the children of all the men and the women who ever walked the earth. That the earth itself and its moon and all the other planets and bodies orbiting the sun will at some point come to hang mournful and lost in a forever night sky once the sun is extinguished.

When that unlimited mass of gas and fire finds its limit and runs out of fuel like an automobile on a desert highway, and the black cold of the eternal void overtakes everything, all living things, all life, all of it will be seized and its energy meticulously and inexorably drained and its frozen husks abandoned to the ghostly nothingness of deathly space.

All the plans in your head, all the recollections of the deeds you have done and all the pangs of remorse about those you have not done, and all the trepidation and the anticipation and the hope for tomorrow, all the many seconds of experience of sentience and consciousness, all of this will whirl away into that monstrous vacuum of eternity and be gone forevermore.

All crushed mercilessly into non-existence.

To return eventually, if time be without end.

But what if even time dies? What then?

All this comes to me in and from those otherworldly sounds from the pianist's pressing upon the keys of an instrument tuned in a way I do not expect, in a way that robs me of the anchor of my musical heritage and memory and sets me adrift into a bleak universe of empty space and darkness.

～

But there is more. Oh, thankfully! There is more!

For the harp, left there to weather when Sir Francis Drake's one remaining ship needed to lighten itself of cargo in order to make the trip back to England, taken up by local peoples as an object of worship and left atop a cliff overlooking the sea, where the oceanic winds played its strings as the sun and the rain and the heat and the cold altered its intonation, producing such supernatural music, the harp gave forth its transcendent performance for a time, however brief in the span of all time.

And some few wanderers from an ancient race heard it and pondered the mystery of which it spoke in the infinitesimal span they had here on this globe.

Those sounds from outside this world, from a place we can never know but which is somehow always lurking just at the fringe of our perception and attention, darkening, deepening the contour of the pattern we make for such a brief time on the fabric of this world, those sounds emerged and were perceived and resonated in the souls of those men long dead, just for a time. As the sounds of this album resonate in my soul now.

And those men long departed understood the sounds they heard as a gift from heaven.

The whole of the story is there.

They heard them and accepted them as testimony of the life of the spirit. As a promise from that other realm, a guarantee of its existence and its shelter from the storm of our world. And doubtless in hearing this message from beyond our realm, from that of the spirits, they were reassured and made glad, as I too find that reassurance in the thought of their happiness in those joyous tidings.

As I settle on that guidepost, I am opened to hearing the strange airs otherwise. I feel myself rising to accept the same gift, to acknowledge the same message, to receive the same promise, and to discern the indescribable beauty that escapes all words and all thought in the very sounds that had plunged me into that void.

The void and the promise are inextricably linked. Twins. One and the same.

BOXES OF BOOKS

IN MY FIRST LONG RESEARCH trip to France, I packed up some of my books in boxes and shipped them from the US. Twelve or fifteen or so big packing boxes.

I had not thought about how I would manage with them in France when they arrived until they actually did. Luckily, a friend with a car helped me load them from the post office to my apartment a few blocks away.

Then, nine months later, I had to change apartments. The old one and the new one were in the same Paris arrondissement, the 13th, one just south of Place d'Italie, the other just north of the metro stop at Les Gobelins, about a 17-minute, 1.3 kilometer walk straight up avenue de Choisy to Place d'Italie, and then up avenue des Gobelins.

My friend with the car was out of town at the time I had to make the move. I decided I would carry all the book boxes from the old place to the new. This was, I determined in my crazed oblate state, consonant with the bizarre ascetic regime with which I had then shackled myself, with the goal of concentrating fully and ferociously on the writing of my thesis—I had begun restricting my sleep to five hours a night and my bed consisted of a thin futon mattress with no frame and no pillow.

Of course, the work had to be done one box at a time, as they were big and bulky, and each box weighed 35-40 lbs. I could have taken the metro for part of the journey—the one stop between Place d'Italie and Les Gobelins—but that would have meant going down and up a bunch of stairs crowded with rushing fellow humans twice each trip, plus negotiating the turnstile and my ticket while carrying a giant box of books. I thought it better just to walk the whole thing.

My first apartment, which was, if I remember correctly, on the fourth floor, at least had an elevator, whereas the new place was on the sixth floor (this, I recall with certainty, as I colorfully cursed all six flights aloud in two languages each time I had to ascend them), and there was no elevator.

As I was doing this in the midst of an unusually hot Paris summer, I thought (the one wise thing that came into my head in the midst of all this foolishness) I should work after the sun went down in order to avoid being melted into the pavement, so I started in the early evening. I somehow managed to get it all done in a night, finishing in the wee hours, and then I slept most of the next day.

When I awoke, I found for a short period of time that I could not get out of bed, my legs were in such agonizing pain. Although I was slightly worried I had permanently crippled myself, which would complicate finishing my thesis according to the schedule I had determined (the only thing that mattered), I nonetheless admiringly compared myself to the Zen Buddhist monk who, in the koan if not in real life, dealt with his fatigue during meditation by ripping off his eyelids.

LES CIMETIÈRES

DO NOT EAT THE ENTIRE DAY. Prepare body and mind ritually. Bring a slab of cheese, some bread, an apple, and a bottle of orange soda. Sit at a bench in the autumn sun for hours and watch people walk by as you eat. No reading or other distractions. Let your nostrils fill with this air and your mind with the thoughts provoked by being in this place. Wipe away the sweat on your brow produced by the brisk walk from the train station. Cool and calm down. Emulate the teachers all around you.

An hour from closing, as the sun nears the horizon and the other visitors have retreated to their homes, fetch a map of the grounds and proceed.

Find the suicided philosopher, whose friends promise never to forget her.

The writer with a photo of her as a young girl with another who is perhaps her sister.

The intellectual couple who lie only steps away from where you chewed your meal and contemplated the living walking among the dead.

The poet interred with the stepfather whom he detested.

The singer whose tomb is covered with subway tickets.

Another writer lying side-by-side with his wife under the blackest of slabs.

The actress with the headstone reminiscent of the hairstyle she wore in the '60s film from which you learned of her art.

The foreign political leader who is visited here by his countrymen from across the ocean.

The wife of the philosopher and the artist you stumble upon while looking for someone else.

Some you seek you will not find in the maze. In a coincidence that must be an augury or a fate or at least a fine literary touch, the shooting star who left a few brilliant pages in his youth and then was extinguished too young in a war, his art condemned eternally to what might have been but was lost, he cannot be found here where the map indicates he should lie.

But you find the one you sought this day, identified simply as "Poète 1896-1963."

Clean the dead leaves and wilted flowers away so that the words can be seen by any who look and polish the stone with your jacket sleeve and some saliva.

As the cold gathers, let it enter you, in preparation. Practice your breathing as the bell tolls and the guards come to fetch you. You can now go off to a warm place and drink a warm drink and entertain warm thoughts.

But now you will recall more easily. That warmth is for but a fleeting moment, some days, perhaps dozens, hundreds, even thousands, but a reckoned number that will soon enough come to its end, and then you will be back in this, the most human and humane city, the one in which we all find permanent residence and a place to lie down and take a load off.

How can any fear of failure, any trepidation in the face of ridicule or shame or exclusion, any worry for tomorrow and the day after that, how can any of that touch you, if you will but return in spirit and in your gut to that stone that today you touched and wiped clean of debris and traced in it the letters of the name of a man that are now all that remains of him?

CASCADE STREET '98

A CINEMA SOMEWHERE NEAR THE BASTILLE, tucked away in one of the side streets. A hole in the wall, a projector, a screen, a place to shelter from the sun and to dream.

I was watching a lot of film, trying to forget something. The something was a fantasy that I had created inside my head about a love story, a random meeting on a subway transformed into a romance and into a life together against everything, against fate and against death.

The fantasy did not come to be, as they typically do not. But I had somehow come to believe, however briefly, that it would, so dramatically committed was I to the poetic life at this strange, magical moment in my tenure on the planet. In the manner of the hopeless optimist who pretends to be a pessimist because he believes perhaps in this way he will fool destiny, I pretended that I had known it all along. If the miraculous thing is not really wanted or expected, perhaps it might then be decreed by the fates as a punishment? *"I do not really think it is possible, and I hope that in expressing that disbelief that it will come to pass just in order to prove my ability to know anything about the future or to gainsay my destiny is non-existent."*

I had kissed her on a bridge over the Seine.

I had held her hand while we two stood beneath that same bridge, near the water's edge, marveling at the fact that the river was there and we were there and all of this was truly happening, as a dream made real.

But it did not come to be, and that truth was coming to nest in my brain, burrowing about, looking for materials with which to build itself a home so that it could rest comfortably there and force me to understand that my will could not budge the world.

In the novels, in the poems, in the movies, events sometimes go otherwise. So, I sought the otherwise.

I knew almost nothing about the film (*La Vie rêvée des anges/The Dreamlife of Angels*) I set out to watch that evening. It was the story of two women. One was my spiritual copy, her gaze firmly downward and her expectations minimal but yet desiring desperately for the dream to come true. She, downtrodden, no one, adrift in the ocean of castaways, stumbles across a well-off lover, and she thinks he can give her the happiness denied her at every turn before he appeared.

But the dream failed here in this cinema world too, and the young woman who was my soul's twin was destroyed by it. Delicate, beautiful, vulnerable flower, pretending to be cold and hard and fierce, but defenseless and decimated and ruined by the deceit of another.

That sadness was, however, not the film's meaning.

The second woman, her friend, seemingly emptily delusional about the reality of the world, too happy for no good reason, works a miracle. She is a saint. She saves the life of a young girl in a coma through the sheer determination of her love and prayer.

And in the film's conclusion, she returns to a life of drudgery and work, and it should be unbearable, and we should know that her friend was right to give up and to remove herself from this horror of failed fantasy and realized defeat and unbearable boredom.

But it is not so. The saint turns to the work with inner joy, aware that love is in the world, though we do not know its workings and it surprises us, always.

There is music accompanying her labor, as she connects innumerable wires to innumerable posts, and it is spiritually elevating, medieval and modern at once, signaling the angels that dance as we turn to quotidian tasks if only our souls can open to mystery as hers abundantly has.

Her smile is without affect or purpose other than to radiate adoration of the marvel of being alive.

We see other women working the assembly line, reaching for the posts and the wires, their eyes tired, yet still shimmering with all the life and the love and the heartbreak and the experience of the years they have had and the years that are to come, the promise of just being alive, breathing, seeing, feeling, ready for anything.

One of these, delicate profile, with heavy, huge eyes, reaches for something. Her head tilts in a way that seems somehow familiar, a way that expresses in just that little movement, that slight incline of her head, the uplift of her brow, something of the weight that has been brought to bear on her in her short life and something of the energy she still has in abundance to carry it. Her arm is scarred, a riposte to the perfect lines of her nose and her mouth. Her life, full of everything, beauty and pain.

My heart fills watching her, watching all of them, this army of feminine soldiers on a crusade for all of life itself.

The song's lyric is "*When I'm asleep, I see nothing, when I'm asleep, I hear nothing.*" A violin recapitulates the melody at the end. It is unbearably, achingly lovely.

As I walk out into the street, the evening is settling in, the glow of the recently departed sun drizzling down on the buildings, and I forsake the train to walk instead the several miles through streets overflowing with life home to my apartment.

I see the dead woman, I feel her loss and her pain and her failure, but I see too the other, the one alive, the one at work, the one going on despite it all.

I see her smile and her shining eyes, and I see the others working alongside her too, with their big eyes and their big hearts, and I hear that music. And I want to be here, right here, walking these cobbled streets at dusk, the traffic quieting as night approaches, following the river, my heart beating, my mind racing, my disillusionment now redeemed by art, ready to go on.

THE ONLY ONE ALONE

WHILE IN A FOREIGN CITY, after a long train ride to come from the vast metropolis where my plane had touched down to this humbler human conglomeration, still hundreds of thousands in population but microscopic by comparison, I walk through a bustling square just adjacent to a college campus.

Fresh-faced students are all around, sitting at the outdoor tables of restaurants and cafés, standing together at the entrances of shops and bookstores, walking in little pods in every direction. Social groupuscules of every set of dimensions, busily chattering and laughing and holding hands and enjoying one another's human warmth and company.

Clearly content, all of them, in their collective project of chasing away from each consciousness the terror of loneliness and solitude, the coldness of our isolation and the seeming impossibility of bridging the space that lies between us, no matter how physically close we are.

I find an open chair and table outside the Café Something or Other. I sit and await the server, who listens, bustles away, and then returns with my espresso. I take a sip and pull my book from the bag I have placed under the table, along with a small notebook and a pencil.

All around me, the warm drone of human vocalization, the ambience of our collectivity. I breathe in the heat of their togetherness, just off there at a slight and easily bridgeable distance, but maintain my haughty separation from their world. I love them, brothers and sisters that they are in our common journey, and recognize my need of them, but I am yet happy where I am.

In the midst of this swarm of togetherness, I am the only one alone, pointedly aware of what I lack and yet in the best of all possible worlds.

WORDS MORE
THAN WORDS

TRYING TO PUT WORDS TOGETHER in such a way as to make the reader cry. To make him weep with joy and pain at the unfathomable richness of being alive. To fill him with such energy that he believes he can leap from a plane and survive, soaring down through the clouds as some featherless and oversized falcon. To arouse in him the terror of standing alone on a moonless plain on an unknown world while things he cannot even comprehend stalk him. To evoke the anger that is set alight in a man when he sees someone attack his flesh and blood and leaps to the child's defense with annihilation in his gaze and his heart.

To make words do those things. What is the secret behind that conjuring?

It must be acknowledged that we make the task harder by talking so often about mundane things. We profane our language daily merely by insisting on speaking it, using it for the banal commerce of the everyday, to pay for the groceries and ask when the package will be delivered and tell the repairman when we will be home to receive him.

It cannot but be weakened and diluted by this use, however unavoidable it is. Even music would be moved to a point of great distance from the austere mountaintop on which it sits if we insisted on using it to communicate to merchants which products and how many of them we desired to purchase from them.

And what is left to be said? Are there any new things to say, or at least new ways of saying old things?

The answer is unclear, the math of how many possible coherent combinations might exist for a finite number of words still unknown.

Has it all been said? Has everything worth writing been written?

It may well be so.

And if so, why write?

Only in the hope of a miracle.

A wild, irrational gesture, a radically unfounded prayer that one can somehow conjure magic from mundanity, even after all the centuries of others doing the same thing and leaving their piles of spells behind them as a warning to the intrepid.

A hopeless act of hope. Hopelessness, hoping despite itself, because to give up entirely is to immediately consign oneself to the ashes.

That is what writing is.

Fishing for miracles.

THE SECRET DEATH

ANY DEATH THAT ANNOUNCES ITSELF in advance is inevitably a more horrible death, at least for the one who dies, than the one that comes of a sudden and discretely removes you, quickly, easily, with no time for the anguish and the preparation for that finality for which one can never, ever be prepared.

For when you find out you have terminal cancer, learn that it is doing its noxious work inside you, you come to know something intolerable. You know that it has already been there for some time, perhaps for years, lurking undetected, evading the screening, causing no pain or discomfort that might alert one to its existence, biding its time, preparing to make itself felt only when the game is so far advanced that a life-changing ordeal is assured, even if somehow death is avoided. Try as you might, in such a situation, you will be unable to avoid that most corrosive of thoughts: *"If only I'd . . ."*

You go to the doctor when you have to urinate too much, or too little, or there is a little discomfort in that area, and he sticks his finger up there and pushes, and there is pressure but no pain. Or your chest hurts—not pain, really, but an impossible to describe pressure or burning—and you have a bit of a sore throat, and you have been eating cough drops for a few weeks but it will not go away, and the doctor listens with the stethoscope and checks your heartrate and blood pressure. And in both cases, the doctor assures you that you are fine.

But he does not *know* that you are fine. This is merely the professional rhetoric of physicians, which most of us are incapable of properly translating.

You see, they tell you things as matter of fact that they cannot know with certainty. When you try to force them to greater honesty, to give you the *odds* that there is nothing seriously amiss given the particular limited knowledge-gathering techniques they employed, they are apt to look uncomprehending, as though you had asked them to demonstrate that the earth is *not* flat.

Respond to a doctor who has just checked your prostate and told you he is sure you do not have an aggressive cancer that you want to know *how* he knows that, and he will say something like "*Well, because I do this a lot, I've seen a lot of patients with your symptoms, and your prostate feels like the prostates of these other men, and none of them have had cancer.*"

Try responding this: "*But that is not knowing, and all those previous cases are not a proof. There is still a chance, I could simply be the first.*"

The doctor has not read David Hume and would not care to hear his argument concerning the imperfect nature of inductive reasoning in any event. There is simply an uncomfortable feeling in the air for a moment, then the doctor will ask you if you have any other questions, and you will shake your head. He will tell you to relax and send you out to the desk to make your co-pay. Then he will move on to the next person in the waiting room.

And you will go home, still lacking the knowledge that you do not have death growing inside you at that very moment.

The economy of medical diagnosis is predicated on statistics. That is, on the calculation of human life as something that can reasonably be thought about as we think about, say, the chance of winning fifty dollars with a lottery ticket.

The patient explains that he is having stomach pain, a strange burning sensation in his upper abdomen that began four days ago, very occasional initially, only perhaps three or four times in a day, and for seconds at a time, and that now occurs every five or ten minutes, with greater intensity.

The doctor palpitates here and there, listens to the patient's breathing, takes a urine sample, checks the vitals that the nurse recorded before the doctor's appearance. Then quickly (and it must be quickly, for there are other patients who must be gotten to), in his mind's eye, he thumbs through the memories he has of other cases, of things he has read, of distant recollections from his residency and medical school work. And in a matter of minutes or even seconds, he determines that the chances are good that this is a case of some gastro-intestinal tract disturbance of minor character, correctable by time and a probiotic or an antacid.

Chances are good.

This phrase could theoretically always be translated into a statistic, even if the doctor is not immediately able to call the precise number to mind. Perhaps the research exists somewhere that shows the number to be, let us say, around sixty-five percent. This means that in nearly seven of ten cases, the diagnosis is accurate, and the patient goes off to obtain his probiotic tablets or antacid medication and in a few days is not even able to conjure up the memory of what the odd burning felt like.

But in more than three of ten cases, the diagnosis is not correct.

In some percentage of this number, probably the majority, maybe even *nearly* all of the remaining cases, the actual cause is still minor and benign, and the patient recovers fully, and usually quickly, despite the doctor's mistaken diagnostic guess.

But in some number of cases, a small number and perhaps a very small number but always a number greater than zero, the diagnosis is badly, perhaps horrifically wrong.

In these situations, the patient has some terrible bacterial infection that, given the extra two days between this visit and the subsequent trip to the emergency room in a squad, is able to effectively cripple his internal organs and bring about his painful death. Or he has an invasive tumor in his stomach that is rapidly expanding and that will, in due course, inevitably, inexorably, colonize his body to the point that it simply surrenders to the tumor, cedes to it, and stops functioning, and the delay in the diagnosis turns out to be of some unknown but significant import.

And in the cruel and stupid *danse macabre* that is the way of nature, the tumor that forced the body to its death will in turn die without the mouth and the stomach of the body it invaded to bring it nourishment. But in fact, it is not even an invader. It is made up of cells of the very body it wants to kill, transformed into little antagonists by the mysterious calculus of random mutation. It is the body turned monstrously against itself, an auto-destruction, a suicide of a particularly sinister variety in which the body becomes multiple and one part of it murders the rest, and incidentally also puts an end to itself.

Do you want a problem of sufficient difficulty to work on for a lifetime, however long that turns out to be for you? *Think on what was in the mind of God when he produced a world that operates according to such a logic.*

BELIEF: A DEFINITION

WHEN YOU SAY, "I BELIEVE," what is it that you are saying, exactly?

What you are *not* saying is that you grasp something with certainty. "I believe" does *not* mean "I know."

The word comes down to us from the Old English "*belyfan*" (to have faith or confidence), and earlier from the Proto-Germanic "**ga-laubjan*" (to hold dear or love), still earlier from Proto-Indo-European "*leach*" (to care for or desire).

"I believe" means "I hold dear." "I esteem." "I have confidence." "I have faith."

"I believe" might just derive its greatest sustenance from its incalculable distance from "I know." When "I believe" is at the greatest possible remove from "I know," it is then at its truest, though it is of course not a matter of truth.

"I believe" may well be equivalent to "I do *not* know and yet I insist, with every fiber of my being."

"I believe," which is to say, "I know that what I believe is not known and cannot be known."

When a thing is true, it is known. I know, then, that what I believe cannot be true. I know reason shows that it cannot be.

And yet I believe. I am convinced of the thing that I do not and cannot know.

Even given my conviction, I do not seek to persuade you of my belief. I do not attempt to bring others to my view. I understand that is their affair, entirely, and I have no business in it.

I have chosen this stance of belief, personally, alone, because of two things that I do know, with complete certainty. The two things that I know are that I am irreparably broken and that the truth cannot be of any help to me in this matter of my brokenness.

I believe because I am broken, because I suspect the whole world is broken, and I wish to be otherwise, and I know of nothing known that can make this so. I accept the unacceptable, which is to say that I believe what can never be known, which is another way of saying that it cannot be true.

I accept it because I do not want to cease to exist. I know that I will die. That is the truth. But the truth is of precisely no use to me in the single matter of greatest import.

I believe because to do so carries me outside of the knowing that all knowing is futile and worthless because it ends in nothing at all.

If I am not to die, I have no other choice but this way, which is the way of "I believe."

This is the way of will, of pure freedom, of escape from what is re-quired of me by that saddest of all paths, the path of the truth, the path I have trod so often and so diligently but that I must abandon when it no longer serves me, as here it so evidently does not.

A BARN AND A BRIDGE

I AM IN A CAR AS I see them. That is already a problem. An error.

Afoot, they would take on vastly different appearances. Were I walking, I would have the leisure to take in the full perfection of these two structures, one of which I am moving past, the other which I am preparing to traverse.

A barn and a covered bridge in the countryside, there together just outside the town in which I live.

A barn and a bridge like those in the paintings, in the old photos and antique books, in the memories of people aged but not yet gone and who therefore can still speak of the memory and make us aware of it.

A barn and a bridge built patiently, lovingly, by the hardened but yet warm and supple hands of men who lived and died and who are now buried within walking distance and whose spirits may well roam the nearby woods on clear autumn nights. Assembled with saws, hammers, and nails, out of good local wood, and painted that hue everyone knows as barn red, a color derived through tradition from the early method of making barn wood last longer by applying a reddish-brown combination of linseed oil, milk, lime, and rust.

Built simply, efficiently, to exacting standards. Built to last and built to please the aesthetic senses.

This barn and this bridge are man-made things, yet they fit this country as perfectly as though they had grown in its soil, from seeds deposited there by the dung of birds flying overhead. They belong in this space. They inhabit it. They do not dominate it. They find a natural place in it, among the fields and the trees and the waterways surrounding, among the people dwelling here. Among the horses and the cattle and the farm work and all their associated sights and smells and sounds.

I imagine sometimes—more frequently than is my preference, but the thought comes to me entirely unbidden—that this might be the last bridge and the last barn of their kind.

Forever.

I fear that this is all going, more rapidly than can be understood from just a glance at the bridge and the barn, and that soon it will be gone. That it is all in the process of dying, that it will soon be no more.

And I fear that the young people I see in the world, who will be here long after I am no more, know nothing of all this.

And I fear that they care still less.

I am afraid that their world, the only world they have ever known, the world of plastics and things moving quickly and impermanence as a universal rule, is whirling rapidly away from this barn and bridge world, and the two worlds have nothing in common and are mortal enemies.

Their world? Let us speak truthfully. *It is* our *world because my kind built it, and the older world into which I was born was someone else's making.*

I am afraid that their world, which we built for them, is more ruthless and more cunning and more powerful than the world of the barn and the bridge. I fear it will crush the world of the barn and the bridge.

People have always come to feel this way as they age and sense the world moving away from them. Perhaps it is nothing more than that. It nonetheless feels true.

Though I did not build it, and though my kind is responsible for the world that is presently attempting to consign it to the dust heap, the world of the barn and the bridge is the world into which I was born.

And it is the world I love with my truest heart.

Into this world, I descended all those many years ago, years that seem days, so close is the beginning in my memory.

The fields in which I ran in the spring and stalked snakes in the growing corn in the summer, sandstone on which I climbed and sang to the lizards that had come out there to sun the lethargy of their cold-blooded bodies away, dusty and winding dirt roads long ago paved, pigs and cows and chickens in a barnyard coated in dandelion, bullfrogs plopping into a pond with clockwork precision in tune with my steps around its edge, strawberries in a garden and a basket in hand, sheets and overalls suspended on a clothesline and casually marking the shape of the breeze, a meandering stream of water gently flowing so cold and clear, two old but still bouncy Airedales chasing squirrels up apple trees bearing pristine fruit, a praying mantis on a rose bush daintily feasting on a Japanese beetle, the courtship call of the cicada on humid summer evenings the most beautiful tone poem ever composed.

The wilds of those woods that I walked as a youth, with myths of my people about what lurked and what magic was done here, stories of the witches that dwelt there during autumn nights and the delightful chill on hearing these tales. At once, fear of things unseen in that dark place and the security of being in the only place it feels right to call home, the ancestral dwelling places out of which our race sprang and that speak to us still in our hearts, however quietly now, and even, here and there, in the shapes of the structures in which our deepest selves dwell.

Gazing at the barn and the bridge, all of this is in my head, and I say a silent prayer that it might last just a little longer, coherent and comforting, in the form of my memory.

And I ask only that I might already be gone before all that goes, finally, and this alien world that is now ascendant becomes the dismal scene of the lives of those unfortunate souls who are never to know the barn and the bridge.

WHEN JOHN CAGE DIED

I THOUGHT ABOUT THE COMPOSER John Cage's fatal stroke as you would think about chance operations, which he used in much of his work.

So many possibilities of what can happen at every moment of one's life, and at each instant the Fates are rolling dice, or consulting their I Ching, or whatever their method is. And the operation each time involves the possibility of death. Each time. The probability is all that changes.

Early in life, only extremely bad luck, at least in the modern industrialized world, gets you the undesired outcome. It is not linear in its alteration. It is slightly higher just after birth than it becomes around the second or third year, when it reaches the lowest point it will attain. Then it slowly starts to climb.

Inexorably, the probability that snake eyes will come up increases. Until finally it is the only outcome that can materialize. At each roll, though, it is possible. Theoretically.

In Cage's case, it came just as he was making tea, on an August evening, less than a month before the completion of his eightieth year. He did not die immediately after the stroke that emerged from the dice throw that evening, but was taken to a hospital, where he perished early the next morning.

It is always unexpected. Always.

Yet it should never be so. We should always be anticipating it, knowing, by the numbers, that it must inevitably come. It is the only certain outcome, terribly determined, fully inevitable.

But we are always taken by surprise.

The thing we have to know is coming always arrives to be greeted with shock and dismay. Now? How? Because the dice came to rest in that position, and the event immediately manifested.

Cage's death manifested as he made tea.

Perfectly appropriate for such a man, an arranger of sounds who had tried to remove his will from the process, and who embraced the mundanity of all creative endeavor. What more prosaic, and yet completely artistic, than the preparation of tea? Even without the elaborate ceremony of the Japanese Zen ritual of preparation and presentation of matcha.

You can almost imagine him laughing, pleased with the form of the affair. How could it have been better had he chosen his final act? The leaves in the container, the hot water into the cups, as every other day at this hour, perfectly commonplace, perfectly composed, and then, on this one occasion, a chance disruption. The descent of the death angel.

Where precisely had he been in the process of preparing the tea? At which step in the rite? I longed to know that detail, which of course cannot be known to anyone who was not there, and perhaps not even to such a person.

Merce Cunningham, Cage's companion, was presumably in the apartment, but that does not mean he could answer the question. Perhaps he had been watching the process. Having seen Cage do it day after day for decades, one suspects he might have been less than attentive. Would he have been able to recite the exact step in the preparatory sequence in which Cage moaned, if he moaned, and dropped the cup, if he did drop a cup, and closed his eyes in a grimace, if he did that, and then dropped to the ground?

Likely not. The details of the momentous chance event almost always escape us because we do not know whether this or that or another moment that is passing before us will matter in such a way. We know most of them will not and we calibrate our attention accordingly. But this habit cheats us of something beyond value.

Is this the precise instant that someone who has shared my life drops dead before me, or is it just another forgettable part of a forgettable day?

How would our lives be different if we truly believed, at every moment, that such a cataclysm were possible, and were accordingly aware and attuned? For surely it is possible.

I had asked John Cage a question once, from the audience after a reading he had done. What did he think of people applauding him? Was this an appropriate response? I thought it a clever, properly Dadaist thing to ask.

He said people could do as they pleased. It simply was not his affair.

⌒

On the night that I heard the news of Cage's death, on the other side of the continent, I immediately walked out the door of my apartment and began to head north. As I walked, I tried to avoid thinking of anything not immediately present in the world around me. The wind, the headlights of cars, the sky overhead, nothing else.

I walked, in the middle of the night, five or six miles, past a eucalyptus grove, all the way to the beach.

Time passed without my attending to it. I had arrived. I sat and looked at the ocean and imagined all the infinite dead in that boundless, black sea, washing up before me in swimming molecules that had been parts of their bodies, touching my eager, warm fingers in their eternal lifelessness and prescience.

Darkness slowly made its way over the waves. I stayed there all night in the sand, listening.

SILVIA AND/AS THE DEVIL

A SPLENDID PIECE OF LIFE SPENT recently with Buñuel's *Simon of the Desert*. I have seen it several times. Each time, one scene absorbs me, and I watch it over and over and over again.

The Devil comes to tempt the Stylite who is out in the desert on his pillar, meditating and praying. Satan takes the form of a sensual young woman, dressed as a schoolgirl, singing schoolyard songs with obscene lyrics. She bares her shapely legs and breasts for Simon in a few shots that defy description.

The actress is Silvia Pinal, a Mexican film icon and the mother of Alejandra Guzmán, a charismatic, throaty-voiced Mexican rock singer whose music I came to know from spending time in Baja California long ago, while I was a graduate student in San Diego. Same distinctively mesmerizing face as her mother.

The images work in concert with the narrative to keep the entranced viewer at least potentially out of the grasp of lust. For, however irresistible this prancing little demon might be, Simon gives us the moral lesson and resists her. He remains stoically on his pillar. Even at the film's conclusion, when the sinfully gorgeous Pinal forcibly takes him away into a modern den of iniquity, a smoke-filled dance hall, he sits quietly and does not fall under the spell. So, the scene is both truthful to the power of the temptation of sin and adherent to the ascetic spirituality of the film's namesake, and the viewer (this one, at least) oscillates in this moment between them.

Many of Buñuel's works were explicitly critical of Christianity, but he was always, in all of his cinematic creativity, precisely the kind of ex-Catholic who never manages to remove the spirit of the Church and its eternal concerns completely from his mind. Fall away from the path, as is our destiny, but do not lose hope! The Church has innumerable methods to bring you back into good standing so you can try again.

I was infinitely thankful for this doctrinal spiritual realism as I sat transfixed before the dazzling Silvia. I took still images of this startlingly powerful short scene in which she tempts both the Stylite and the viewer, not least because she was so breathtakingly beautiful in her youth, but also because of the peerless composition of the shots. In a better age, there were genius filmmakers like Buñuel, and I would prefer to see every one of his films thrice before I would waste my time watching anything made by anyone still alive.

There is no doubt that Pinal was bewitched by his genius. When he was asked to do a cinematic adaptation of *Journal d'une femme de chambre* shortly after this film, he agreed, with the intention to do it in Mexico with Pinal as the lead. The film's producer, however, demanded it be shot in France. Though she did not speak French, Pinal was prepared to move there, learn the language, and do the film for free just to continue working with Buñuel.

The stark black and white in the contrast of her outfit and her skin, her playful manner and posing, the miracle of these few seconds of motion and form and sound, captured on film, and now gone forever but for that technological miracle.

Silvia Pinal recently left us, at ninety-three years of age, God bless her soul. Her daughter Alejandra, who is my age, was still three years unborn when she made this film.

I hate the thought that a day will come when these miraculous images will no longer endure and no one will ever again be able to experience the total aesthetic joy and vigorous spiritual exercise they bring me every time they transmit themselves into my consciousness.

BEDTIME EPIPHANY

NIGHTLY, IT MANIFESTS.

The hour informs me that the day must conclude, my body tires, my mind sets on the preparations for sleep. All the little operations required are carried out. Check the locks, turn out the lights. I arrive bedside.

As I settle into the same posture to which my body conformed at its genesis, while still in the womb, a strange spell overtakes me.

The promise of ideas, of tomorrow's work, buzzes to life in my head, as I endeavor to sail off into the world of dream. The satisfying fatigue of my body is welcomed by a now humming mental prescience of things to be written that I somehow did not write in all the hours I was awake.

How did I accomplish so little today? This is the pest that appears and nags my somnolent being back away from the abyss on which I had been teetering.

Some nights, though I fight it viciously, it is so overwhelmingly powerful that it picks me up from my fetal position and deposits me seated on the edge of the bed, then maneuvers my hand over to the nightstand to grasp the smart phone that charges there, and forces me to record some notes concerning the urgent shards of ideas that have come into my head in the minutes just before unconsciousness.

But is it so? Have I really not done the work that day if I resist the daimon that insists I wake and capture those ephemeral impressions that are haunting my impending sleep?

Perhaps it was required, all the sitting and staring, the delays and the distractions, all the things I did today instead of writing words and sentences and paragraphs, all the other things that are seemingly unconnected, and that yet might be the work itself.

I am unsure how the work is done. Certainly, I know of the moments when my hands become possessed of a life all their own and rapidly peck away at the keyboard, and words appear on the screen, and my mood grows cheerful, and I am happy beyond happiness to be doing what I am presently doing, because something that one could reasonably call "the work" is apparently happening.

I know precious little though about what sparks those occasions, fleeting as they are, and far outweighed in quantity by the anxious periods of half-despairingly flipping through piles of papers and books in search of something completely unknown, pouring myself coffee in an endless stream, hoping for a surge of energy that I know was already depleted hours ago.

What is the science of the creation of that mental space in which one does the writing?

The work is a mystery. No one knows what it is, how to define or teach it, how to ensure that it will happen in a particular place at a given time.

Sometimes, too often, when you think you are doing it, feverishly slogging away, fingers dancing, soul ablaze, you produce nothing that will survive the following day's furious revising.

Other times, when you think you are not doing it, when you are distracted by the crack near the kitchen window and wonder whether it will need to be repaired soon, and then start looking for the handyman's number just in case, and stumble upon some other scribbling from another day instead, a note that should not have been where you found it but there it was, and you make an unanticipated mental connection between that cryptic note and something that you understand to be profound, that is when the most important work is being done.

Perhaps tomorrow's work, which I cannot yet perceive, has its germ in the moments I spend in the dark, under a blanket, my arms wrapped around my upper body, my hands warming at my shoulders, as the glow of sleep settles down on me as a dust gently moved by the evening wind.

VISIONS IN TWO CARS

A TWO-LANE COUNTRY road somewhere in eastern Tennessee.

A sporty new car, going too fast, with a family inside, young children, in the age when seat belts were new and no one in the country used them.

Another car approaches.

It cannot be known what is in the head of the driver who comes toward you in the facing lane, as the two of you abide by the white line separating eastbound from westbound, northbound from southbound, and all the in-betweens.

Generally, he is competent and clear-headed, and everyone is lucky, and the numbers tell us that mostly the cars pass one another, the drivers perhaps exchanging a glance in the instant of nearest proximity. Both then speed off in opposite directions, never again to come within 100 miles of one another. As asteroids floating in the space between Mars and Jupiter, and almost never colliding, their tiny size and that immense void calculating against the probability.

But rarely, it comes to pass. On this day, it did so.

What was in the other driver's mind, this day? It might have been the fog of alcohol, the emotional cloud of a breakup with a girlfriend, a moment of fatalism and recklessness, a drunk in a car racing along a strip of country road, attending to nothing but the distress in his heart and his desire to stop the pain.

He passes no other car for a full twenty minutes, and then, fatefully, as measured and determined by the physics of the universe from the beginning of time, comes the other car. The one containing a family, the husband and the wife, the two children, one a mere baby in the arms of the grandmother of the man, who is driving his young family home after a visit with other relatives.

The unknown driver collides with the family's car, in which I am a passenger, a boy of only a few years of age.

My mother's arm reaches for me and stops my progress forward on impact, perhaps saving my life, at least preventing major injury. I am hurt, but slightly, a cut on the mouth from the seat, and scared half to death.

But alive. Miraculously. Alive, when I might very well have been dead.

Alive.

I was too young to produce clear memories of the event, though some vague distillation of the experience has been with me for as long as I can remember. All the crucial details I learned later from others. This distance does not diminish my sense that I was saved that day, caught at the cusp of the next world and pulled back into this one.

～

Twenty years or so later, I am in another car.

The driver, my friend, is nineteen years old. I am all of twenty-two or so, and we are going to a party somewhere, with others like us. We have gotten a head start on the festivities, and both of us are more than a little drunk. In our part of the world as it was when we were that age, this was not at all an uncommon thing.

We speed along. As the car hurtles forward, a premonition comes to me.

I see this car in wreckage, and I see the ruin of my friend strewn among the shards of metal that once moved so sleekly and swiftly. I see his lifeblood run out and away in rivulets down the asphalt.

I hear the lamentations of his family, and especially I hear the weeping grief of his mother, who cherished this boy, loved him with all her aching heart, gave him everything he wanted because she loved him so, and who with the boy's father paid for this car that he so avidly and eagerly drove to the rendezvous with his own death.

I see her bury that boy, her son, my friend, untimely, senseless. She is so lovely, and it is heart-rending to see her cry out her anguish at the loss of her beautiful child, now no more of this world.

Sobered, I get out of my friend's car and close the door as we arrive at our destination. The alcohol buzz is gone, as if by some magical intervention that removed the chemicals stupefying my neurons in a flash.

I swear to myself never to be in that car with him at the wheel again.

Somewhere, just a few years later, the premonition came to pass, and he perished in that car. Just as I saw it that day. In every awful detail.

～

I still wonder why it has been given to me to escape this end not once, but twice. Perhaps all lives of more than a few years must inevitably be marked by such visitations. Their commonality does not make them less remarkable. For each person, when he realizes they have happened, they are as lightning strikes to the soul, marking him forever.

I read of a man in New York City who stayed up late watching Monday Night Football, his favorite team the Giants playing out west in Denver, and because the game ended in the early morning hours on the East Coast, he overslept the next morning. The morning of September 11, 2001. As he made his way late to his place of employment (the North Tower of the World Trade Center), a plane flew into the building, and he realized that failing to hear his alarm clock had saved his life.

We cannot be assured of what comes next. Only that, eventually, our death is the thing that comes next. But something in the universe allies with us, on rare yet not entirely uncommon occasions, to push back that inevitable meeting, through means we cannot fathom, according to a logic we will never know.

DIE FRÖHLICHE WISSENSCHAFT À PARIS

HOW CAN DEATH claim me as its own?

As I sit here, full of youth and spiritual fire and the ideas of this book on the table before me, a book that I would have written if only I could, energized by caffeine and the sheer joy of the roads without end extending from where I sit into the world to come, it is impossible.

How mundane, to die. How banal. How expected. How *menschlich*.

It cannot be so for me. Not now, not in any future, so long as the fire of these seconds, these minutes and hours remains in my brain.

So long as I can still taste the bitterness of the tiny white cup's black liquid, and the sweetness of the tab of chocolate and the packet of brown sugar, and the warm, flaky crust of the croissant.

So long as I can feel the book in my hand, the crisp pages as I turn them, so long as I can see my scribbled notes in the margin.

So long as I hear the cars and the buses and the taxis and the motor scooters in the plaza before me, so long as I smell the exhaust that hovers momentarily before dissipating into the surrounding air.

So long as I see the students walking to and from the various *lycées* and *collèges* and *universités* spread throughout the neighborhood, so long as I hear the low buzz of their chatter and the peals of their laughter.

So long as I sense the flitting presence of the waiters gliding soundlessly through the café, drinks carefully balanced, aprons lightly soiled but still elegant.

So long as the pungent odor of cigarette smoke trails around the corner from the two young women at the table partially obscured from my view, revealing just enough to see here a leg beneath a skirt, there a slender arm reaching out to take the cup offered by the server, while the sun paints the whole street scene before me in vivid hues, and the world turns, and the universe continues its expansive journey at infinite speeds into the void.

Tu trembles, carcasse! Embark!

THOSE JUGGLING FIRE AND THOSE IN THE PATH OF HURRICANES

I CAN REMEMBER THE DRIVE across the border from San Ysidro into Mexico as though I last did it yesterday, though it has been more than two decades now, and doubtless everything about the particulars has changed since then.

Slowing to allow the patrol to briefly scan your still-moving car, just to conduct the instantaneous visual test to determine whether you are sufficiently suspicious to require stopping. When no one looks longer than a second or two and you continue on through the checkpoint that is mostly not a checkpoint, you accelerate back up to cruising speed and then follow the ramp around on to a main boulevard.

As you make this roundabout, a panorama of the city of Tijuana presents itself to your vision. Not entirely unlike other cities you have seen and yet possessed of its own unique energy. You coast along exhilarated, barely aware of the car's tires on the road, as though breathing a different kind of air, somehow more fragrant and intoxicating, and affected by a greatly reduced gravitational force. Through the permeable barrier between the known and the unknown.

Then, at the first light off the freeway, they come out to greet you. They want to wash your windows sometimes.

And sometimes they are juggling fire.

They appear in a blur of motion, in seconds putting the flame to their batons, climbing precariously up on flimsy ladders or balancing on stilts, meticulously performing their well-practiced act, then extinguishing the batons and rushing about to collect coins from the cars before the light changes to green and all the potentially paying customers hurry off to their business.

And there are children with them, and sometimes they are children themselves. They often come from Oaxaca and Veracruz and Tabasco, far to the south and the east, from a part of the country that might as well be on Pluto when one compares it with the borderland.

From dusty, narrow roads traversed by but a few cars a day, and the slow, quiet parade of country people who could have stepped from the pages of a work of history, to noise-polluted streets bordered by seas of plastic bottles and drunkards sleeping it off and an occasional pool of blood, and a whirlwind of traffic and seedy commerce and seedier transgressions and outright crimes and the full-on depravity of our species in its stomach-turning splendor.

One cannot look on those innocent babies, made too rapidly into something else, something unnatural, rushing to perform for coins at a traffic light in a city far from their home, without feeling as though this world might be a homeless world, an impossible and merciless world, a world wholly devoid of and unfit for love. I do not say it is true, but it becomes easier to suspect it might be when one witnesses the performance of such disheartening dramas.

As inevitably as the dismal condition of the fire jugglers impresses itself on me when I am in Mexico, sitting in a car yards away from them, it just as effortlessly fades from my consciousness when I am elsewhere. Or rather when I am in other places where no fire jugglers in other guises are present.

They sprang into existence again in my mind today as I was watching video from Gulf Coast Florida, desperate images of the devastation produced by a hurricane, of people of every station in life left soaked and destitute, their cars and houses and every material belonging swept away in hellish wind and water, by a force of the natural world against which our vaunted intelligence and technology is nothing.

I thought anew of the impossible, merciless, loveless, and for these desperate men and women now quite literally homeless world that produces the fire jugglers and the victims of hurricanes alike.

I prayed that they be comforted, that they find shelter and warmth and help and love. I prayed it with a sentiment at once hopeful and despairing, or rather alternatingly so, now with sadness and a terrible and oppressive agony, and now with confidence in the promise that the arc of the universe does indeed bend toward the healing of such wounds.

Those hostile to religious faith are contemptuous of the calls of the faithful for prayers for the suffering in such times. "Too easy, and too inconsequential," they say. "*Do something real!*"

It is true. Material help is needed. But not instead of prayer. Indeed, we can never know with certainty that material aid is not itself a manifestation of the success of prayer. At the very least, we are forced to acknowledge that in at least some cases the prayer contributes to the motivation to act in other, more tangible ways.

And perhaps the prayer is not only for comfort and aid to those suffering, but also a cry by the anguished speaker of the prayer to change his own spirit. A request to be made by powers beyond him—for he has proven only too incapable of achieving the outcome on his own—into someone capable of more and deeper charity and brotherly love, someone who does not utterly, effortlessly forget the fire jugglers and the hurricane-pursued as soon as they are no longer before his eyes.

Someone who, when suffering comes to him, as it must, says aloud "*What a gift, these tribulations! How blessed I am, and how much more compassion should I have for those not nearly so lucky, to be* presented with challenges that are so easily superable, instead of those closer to the gravity faced by those juggling fire on the street for coins and fleeing hurricanes that have left them naked against the elements. And even when such unbearable burdens come to me, may I somehow find a way to sing a song of gratitude to this world that so cruelly forsakes me."

DEATH DEPICTED

WE ARE CONSTANTLY TRYING TO forget death and the suffering that inevitably accompanies it, both for the one who dies, in his melancholic meditation on it and if his end is physically painful, and for his loved ones, no matter how he should meet his end. So long as we are young and not gravely ill, the task of forgetting is easily accomplished.

And happily so! Holding it at bay sufficiently to get about one's business is a requirement of living.

But when it is put too far out of mind, our lives inevitably tend toward delusion, and the inescapable end only intensifies in its catastrophe if too completely forgotten.

To keep this rarefied realm of the numinous—and that is what dwelling in death is—always ready to hand, as a means to quickly returning himself to the awesome truth in those times when his thoughts strayed into the comfortable lie that death was not coming for him, the writer Georges Bataille carried with him a photograph.

It depicted something unutterably, fantastically terrible. It was an image of a man in the process of being subjected to the Chinese execution technique known as *lingchi*, or "slow slicing," in which the condemned is put to death over an extended period of time by a series of cuts to the body.

In this horrifying image of another human destroyed, and specifically in the look on the face of this dying man as his life left him, as he understood in the only visceral way such things can be understood that death was indeed here for him now and that there would be no later, Bataille thought to achieve a way into the simultaneously terrifying and transcendent truth of death.

I will not reproduce the image here. Every possible viewer should have the responsibility of making the decision of seeing it or not seeing it. It can be found if one cares to do so, or it can be left safely secluded, as one wishes.

But I have seen it.

It is a harrowing experience just to look at the expression on that man's face as pieces of his flesh are removed with the action of a blade and to wonder what might be transpiring in his consciousness at that instant and to know that what is suffusing his being is something beyond anything you can imagine.

Death is always the limit of experience. It is only experienced once, by each of us, and so the occasion cannot be related to anyone, for we are no more for this world when it is over. But Bataille believed there was a power in this image to at least partially leap over that communicative impossibility and bring to the viewer something of the feared thing otherwise unapproachable.

Was he right? Did it work? Did keeping the photo available make accessible this indescribable space of transcendence? I am unaware if he ever answered these questions.

As a young man, more intrepid and less cautious about moral rules than I am now and admiring of some if not all of Bataille's ideas, I tried to copy his example, putting an image of similar existential gravity into my own wallet.

I have never told anyone of this until this writing. Perhaps I should be ashamed of having done this. There are times when I feel just that shame, but allow me at least the effort to defend myself.

I meant no trivialization of what had happened to the anonymous man who was meeting his demise in the image. It was not my intention to objectify him and his experience for a trivial motive or end of my own. I took the image of his ordeal with the utmost seriousness. What I wanted was for my compassion for what he was there realizing, and for all of us who must follow him, to somehow become sufficiently profound that it might thrust me, emotionally and philosophically if not materially, into his shoes, thereby sloughing off the dull insensitivity we have about the world-ending disaster of death in much of what transpires in our lives and enabling me to enter a more conscious, more empathetic, more compassionate and loving mode of existence.

I loved this man I did not know in his moment of death, and I pitied him. I desired to somehow make his end my own, both to give him a measure of comfort but also to share in a part of his exalted status as one who in the photo was preparing to cross the barrier that is for all of us our primal terror.

I was, at the time I engaged in this experiment, wandering godlessly, so it was easy for me to avoid thinking too hard about any Christian injunctions about such dallying with such forces. I knew that Bataille had himself been a fervent Catholic as a young man, and I hoped that some residue of that had remained with him later in life when he was engaged in so many activities that seemed so clearly contrary to the faith. Those who worship the Devil unavoidably acknowledge in doing so a belief in the existence and the nature of God, and they are easier to bring back into the fold than those whose materialism is so complete that they deny the existence of either.

I knew too of the use in Christianity of the *memento mori*, the anticipation of one's own coming death through symbols of human finitude, that can be found in the presence of the image of the human skull and skeletons in Christian art and funereal design. In some settings, the skulls are real ones, as in a little chapel I once visited in Évora, Portugal, with the charming name *The Chapel of Bones* (*Capela dos Ossos*). It is built of the bones and skulls of local medieval residents exhumed by the Franciscan friars who established the chapel.

I only looked at the photo a handful of times in the several years it resided in my pocket. I neither spoke of it nor showed it to anyone. It was my private methodology for attempting to rip myself away from complacency when it got so thick that my movements slowed and I knew I was drifting dangerously away from an essential element of my life.

The first time or two that I gazed at it, it was as if I were being vigorously slapped in the face by a strong man. Those times, it did the work I desired it to do—to effectively snap me out of somnambulism and force me to become more awake, however briefly. It inspired me those few times to try to do something to affirm this truth, to extend it beyond the instant at which my eyes grasped the image, to live with it before me even after I had put it away.

It is difficult to say precisely what we do know about the death of the other. But whatever it is, it is certainly not the experience of death itself. Again, to die is something one can undergo but once, and we cannot use the experience as a basis for comparison to the experience of others in the same way that we can, for example, know something of what other people are going through when they suffer pain and illness, having gone through them ourselves. Though each human being is called, in Martin Heidegger's terms, to "take upon itself" its own dying, there is a sense in which we can say that a human being does not truly experience even his own death. There is no being there any longer at the moment of the experience to experience it.

It is precisely the fact that we are unable to reflect upon and understand our own deaths in this experiential sense that makes the death of others, which we cannot experience but which we can witness and continue to puzzle and marvel at after the event, all the more astonishing. I wanted to test the limits of this astonishment, to see what element of the truth of the experience might be available in this way.

The test failed. I was never sure what that something that would affirm the truth of the experience in the longer term was, and for that reason I was never sure I was doing anything that might even potentially accomplish it. I am unable to say that looking at the image helped me achieve any more insight into matters of ultimate value. Nothing permanent in me changed as a result of my knowledge that this radiating talisman was in my pocket.

Then, over time, even the slight promise offered by the first few such experiences leaked out of the process. It no longer worked at all, even in the limited way of the first few times.

Death did not greet me there. No sacredness. No outside. No beyond. Only a picture of a horror that became a banal mundanity in the crude fact of becoming a picture. A picture that degraded as it sat folded in the heart of my wallet, crushed by the weight of my body sitting on it, until it was barely even discernible as what I knew it to be.

I eventually removed the image from my wallet and shredded it, feeling a bitter remorse, as though I had irreparably sullied the disappearance from this world of the man depicted through my act. I asked for his forgiveness as I destroyed the photo that represented but did not capture the end of his life.

Was the failure due to the image itself, for proving incapable of doing what Bataille claimed his did?

Or was it mine, for believing any image could do such a thing in the first place?

A TREE FALLS

I HAD A TREE CUT DOWN.

It had long towered over our house, at the side on which all the bedrooms are situated. On starless winter nights, the wind would roar like a host of demons from the west, and the massive tree would move and bend and shake in the darkness. And I would lie awake and think of my children sleeping in those rooms, below the menacingly animated tree, and I knew it would have to be done.

But it was such a majestic thing, this tree.

It rose with haughty dignity, perfectly constructed beauty. It challenged my ever-wavering will, defied my anemic ability to plan for its end.

How many years had it been there? Perhaps as many as I have been alive. Who then was I to choose the fate of such a splendid and aristocratic being?

I made excuses.

It gave us shade from the burning sun. It exquisitely colored the ground with its shed leaves every fall, and with its new seed in the spring. It would require a profound effort, physical and spiritual, to take it down. Perhaps it would even be in the attempt to fell it that something would go catastrophically wrong and only then would the opportunity finally manifest for the massive body to fall into and destroy our house. I would never be able to bear it if my desire to eliminate this perceived threat were to be the cause of the transformation of that threat from hypothetical to actual.

I put it off.

Then one day, finally, inexplicably, for no apparent reason, I pushed the plan forward. I acted to achieve the tree's demise.

The crew came and solemnly went to work. They used machines to reach into the tree's heights, removing its crown bit by bit, the branches falling into a small forest on the lawn. Then, having thinned and shortened it, one man in the truck, armed with a chainsaw, methodically cut off huge chunks of the trunk, and others attached a chain to pull the pieces off.

The pieces of this vast tree were themselves so great in size that they left wide and deep depressions in the earth where they fell, and I could feel the impact, or so I believed, on the other side of the driveway as I looked on.

It took the better part of a day for a group of three men with powerful technology to surgically bring down this titanic living entity without disturbing any of the human dwellings sitting nearby. I watched almost the entire process, standing like a penitent or an accused man awaiting judgment, breathless and awed.

It was just a tree, I told myself. Just a tree.

The crew took a break after they had completed the work of felling it. They drove away to another job site for a while, telling me they would return shortly to gather up the fragments of the tree's body, pile them on a truck, and haul them away.

During their absence, I sprang into action, driven by nothing the slightest bit more rationally comprehensible than the force that had finally compelled me to call them in to cut the titan down. I hurriedly gathered up a few of the pieces of the fallen tree that were small enough for me to carry. They were crescent-shaped wedges cut out to allow physics to do the work to bring the vast being that had dwelt in our presence for as long as we have been in this house to lie humbled on the earth, then to be disintegrated and relegated forever to a time past and not to come again.

I had no understanding as to why I was doing it. I felt charged with a duty that emanated from outside of me. I whispered prayers as I gathered the pieces. I started to weep profusely, and I asked for forgiveness.

I stored the pieces of the trunk of this once regal living entity in the shed, promising myself, and the tree, that I would keep them as long as I live in this house.

There they lie, grave markers, remnants, wordless epitaphs, all that remains of this sacred being that died by my order.

IRRETRIEVABLY, INEVITABLY

EVERYTHING IS FALLING INTO RUIN, and this is terrible because it is all lost, and it cannot be retrieved or rebuilt.

The train of decay is slow but unrelenting, proceeding at a constant low velocity, heedless of any of the many foolish efforts we make to stop or slow it. The whole of it, all that we have ever done and will ever do, all is doomed to fall to pieces, to fail to endure for more than a blink of the universe's eye. Labor and struggle as we will, none of it will abide.

This is terrible. Nothing more dreadful could even be imagined except by beings still more dismal and awful than we are.

But it is also our redemption because it means nothing matters, and therefore nothing that anyone else does is any more important than what we do.

If I spend my day tinkering with a text no one else will ever care about at all, and reading aimlessly, and learning to play just a few more notes of Bach, or if I suspend the idea of getting work done altogether and pass the time while the sun hangs in the sky walking to the park with my wife and my child and kicking a ball and running and climbing on a rock, it is time exactly as well spent as the time spent by anyone else in the history of the species.

For the libraries they write that I do not, and the knowledge they gather that I do not, and the music they make that I do not, and the work they do that I do not, all of it will just as surely wither and disappear in the sands of time as everything that I do. All equally worthless by the ultimate calculation.

There is no debating this. It is transparently true to anyone who considers it honestly and fearlessly. It is a truth so invigorating and total that it crushes all would-be opposing claims into dust . . . with raucous laughter.

And even if there is some calculus of the days of our lives, even if the sum is not zero but some other figure, the calculator lies forever beyond our ken, and we know next to nothing of his methods. How wrong-headed the Puritans were, to be troubled by their ignorance of their fate in the next world. It is in the hands of a power that eludes you utterly. You might just as well lament your inability to predict where you will be in ten years and what will have befallen you between now and then. It is fated, it is predetermined, and you are a child who plays no part in the determination. From your child's eyes, it cannot matter.

It will save us, in the end, this bitter knowledge of the pointlessness of any effort to make something lasting of our own volition. Our salvation is in our utter uselessness. Our strength is our helplessness. We are completely and joyously free by virtue of the gloriously shattering fact that nothing that we can ever do will matter in the slightest.

All praise the *nihil* that is *omnia*!

FIREFLIES

THE LUXURIANT HEAVINESS of the early evening August air deep in the Susquehanna Valley.

I recall similar dusks when I was a boy in another place, so far away now in miles and years. But this eternal moment is still here, now that I have children with whom to live it again.

Two nights, a decade apart, separating the youth of first one, then the second beautiful, miraculous child who came to grace my life, gifts I will never deserve.

We turn on the garden hose to water the flowers and then take turns chasing and spraying one another with it. The loves of my life, first one, then ten years later, her sister squeal with delight, shrieking in their efforts to evade the ropes of cold water, then cackling as they take the hose and pursue me across the grass.

The sun has settled below the horizon, its faint glow still visible. Darkness warmly encroaches from all around, a dark not menacing or fearful but embracing, a caress of humid air slowly cooling, an invisible heavenly host descending to remind we three that we are loved and protected.

The fireflies have appeared, their tiny pointillism painting the air around us with a merry, sacred glow. There is still enough light, just enough, to see them hover, black dots, in the air when their lights are extinguished, but in time they will be invisible save for those flickering instants when they activate their bioluminescence.

How are they possible, these living things that somehow combine oxygen with various chemicals inside their bodies and produce a light that is yet cool enough for them to survive its burning in their innards? And how are we, strange creatures that marvel at the fireflies and inquire and explore and eventually discover precisely how they can make the light they make and why?

An unfathomed mystery, all of it. Compelling and enchanting.

Our yard is a bejeweled throne room, shining with royal splendor, the aristocracy of this world we make up, the parent and the child, sharing our flickering, transitory time on this globe together, unified in blood and in love and in overflowing, glorious spirit.

My child and my child, my children, my babies. The inexpressible love I have for you. These words do not approach it. They are the best I can do in this doomed enterprise of language.

Much better for us to simply inhabit our mutual love as together we excitedly go from one corner of the yard to another, drawn by the glowing, floating beings that make their slow way through the low-lying air, in search of something we do not reckon, gently reaching out to cup this one and then that one, careful not to harm the tiny denizens of some unknown heaven, and I hold my hand out to you to let them crawl the length of the extended finger and then, to your amazement, to take wing again and return to their inscrutable quest.

You ask me if this is the first night the fireflies have come out.

"I believe it is."

"Do they get thirsty?"

"Probably."

"But won't the water put out their light?"

"No, I don't think we have to worry about that. They know how to keep that from happening."

Our cats, buried next to the fence where they shelter under a small tree, receive a drink of water from you. "They might get thirsty too," you reason.

You are already integrated into the world unseen, you understand that our spirits mingle with those of our beloved fellows no longer here, we who remain to dance and play and laugh and love for them in their absence.

You who changed your course, left your star, took off your wings, and traveled from the other world to be here with us, you came to warm these shared moments with what you found in those fireflies, the fire of eternity, and you are the justification of my life.

CATERPILLAR AND HAWK

WHAT AN INVENTION.

Two wheels, with a metal skeleton joining them, and two other wheels, attached to the first two and operated by a chain mechanism powered by human legs. With this simple machine, we attain speeds several times faster than most of us can run, and we can maintain them much longer because of the economy of the machine's design.

I move on such a contraption, along a wooded trail.

Overgrown vegetation crowds in from the edges, reducing the navigable roadway to six feet across. Euphoric after a half hour at a brisk pace, I ride with tunnel vision, focused on the ground before me, not oblivious to what crowds the periphery of my vision, but concentrated on the patch of gravel a few feet in front of my front tire. Vast fields of decaying corn stalks spread out as far as the eye can see just beyond the bushes and trees that line the bike path, but they are not part of the world I inhabit in my hurtling across gravel atop my wheeled machine.

I sweat. The muscles in my legs are singing a joyous ode to life. The sunlight is blocked by trees overhead, and the wind rushing by cools my perspiration as it oozes out of the pores in my skin. A perfect universe of energy and motion.

Then I spy something small, dark, and ever-so-slightly moving in the band of my visual concentration. A fuzzy black caterpillar makes its way across the path and will be crushed beneath my wheel unless I take evasive action.

Instantly, without thought, my hands perform the needed operation with the handlebars, the front wheel turns delicately, and I pass by the tiny living miracle, leaving it to go about its essential business. It must chew leaves and grow into a butterfly that will spread the pollen of flowers so they can proliferate and release oxygen and be devoured by other things that will be devoured by still other things and so the chain will go on.

I am still thinking of the caterpillar's role in the chain when a rapidly moving object zips into my vision, descending from the left out of the trees in an arc before passing yards in front of me, then maintaining its trajectory for a few seconds there, allowing me a precious glimpse of its majesty just before it ascends in a beauteous curve back up into the sky. A red-tailed hawk, its wings mechanisms far more exactingly made than my bike's wheels and gears, its tail fanned in a work of art finer than anything my fellows will ever devise, its eyes trained as tiny scanners linked to a wondrous computer of cells inside its head, pursuing prey.

I am suddenly moved by a strange emotion. Envy, of a sort, that I and my race have distanced ourselves so determinedly from the world in which the hawk exists without effort, but an envy polished into a brilliant sheen by a greater admiration for the hawk's very existence, a worshipping of its elegance and its aesthetic completeness, its speed, its beauty, its seamless fit to the air in which it glides.

And something else. A fuller appreciation of the lowly caterpillar I have just avoided crushing. I had mused, in dodging it, on its place in the order of the universe. Now the abstraction is made concrete. The hawk that just passed so regally before my admiring gaze can be because the caterpillar is. And the reverse is also true. The mere idea of the chain of life has come to life before me. The skeleton of its manifestation inside my head as a thought is hung with the flesh of the world in which I am moving, by the palpable reality of the caterpillar and the hawk.

All of it is required. All of it.

And I too, for how else will the observation be made?

SEA OF CORTEZ

WE WALK DOWN OFF THE ROCKS, onto the sand, then into the sea.

It is astonishingly warm, the air drenched in a moist heat unlike anything one like myself, born and bred in northern climes, has ever felt before. The one with me is the love of my life, the woman who will one day become my wife, and later the mother of my children. The one I love, the only one, the one, the only one.

We are here, swimming in the Sea of Cortez, together, in the sun, our skin bronzed and salty, our spirits contented.

Together, we frolic, we lounge about, we love, we are alive as two who have found an end to the separation and aloneness of being and who will not ever go back to walking in solitude until one or the other is torn from this world by death. We eat ceviche with shrimp and drink cold beer, and we are drunk with happiness just to have arrived in this place, here, now.

Yesterday, we ran into the sea, finding the beach empty, thinking we had it all to ourselves. But as we entered the water, something unexpected happened.

We looked at one another. What is that? Do you feel it?

We both thought, for an instant, that something had gone drastically wrong, that our brains had failed, each of them as one, at the same time, and that some illusion had overcome us both. Odd sensations, unrecognizable as anything but alien at first, then translated eventually into signals of pain by the confused nerve cells in our bodies.

I looked at her, and she at me. As one, we two ran, silent, from the water, and then we exploded in laughter. Only then did we look at the sign on the beach, which alerts swimmers to the dangers of jellyfish infestations of these waters during certain times of the day.

The stings only heightened our sense that we inhabited a world of rare perfection and intensity. That we were chosen and privileged and should not for a moment forget to feel gratitude for such undeserved grace.

Today, we are warier and check the water gingerly before entering, but we chortle at yesterday's misadventure, bonded still more closely together by it. Today, the jellyfish stay in the depths, and they leave the delicious part of the sea along the shoreline to us.

We swim out a few meters and we float, suspended in the pristine salt water, fearless, immortal, protected by a love without bound or limit.

JUSTIFICATION

I HAVE ALREADY ADMITTED THAT THE SENSA-
TIONS, the experiences, the states of consciousness that are the
object of my writing are outside the frivolous game of writing.
They cannot be captured, reexperienced, nor even satisfactorily
represented by my words, or by any other words. The whole project is a failure from the beginning.

It is sacredness I pursue. But sacredness is an experience, fleeting
like the wind, to be had, never to be captured.

Why write about it?

To scream "No!" in the face of the end.

To etch little signs that might outlive me and that might, just perhaps, be seen by other eyes and thereby transmit the symbols that
live in the signs into other minds, thus stretching the experiences
that are my life beyond the inevitable point of time at which my experience will cease and my mind will be entropically transformed
into entities that are not me.

To make a desperate, doomed claim at foreverness.

To assert one final time, in a despairing shriek, my life's desire to
go on.

Not my life alone. Life itself pushes me to this. It is the force and
the energy and the magic and the sheer unlikeliness and logical
improbability of what inhabits me right now, as I write these lines,

seeking to leap from the brain producing the thoughts and the fingers translating them into keystrokes into another, more permanent mode of existence.

I write because life makes me. Writing is not life. Every writer knows that and a part of him always wonders if he is wasting precious time in which he might be living instead of sitting frustrated in front of a sheet of paper or a screen, struggling to find the phrase needed. Yet it is not a contradiction to say that the desire to live is what makes me steal time from my life to write.

While I wrote this, something was happening. Something unknown, yet that must always be known. My death was approaching. It was creeping closer and closer, looming nearer and nearer with each page, with each word. Its precise form obscure, but its outline and its presence undeniable.

Perhaps it was coming—perhaps it is coming, right now, as these words are being translated from my brain through my fingers into the keyboard and then this computer file—in the form of a malignancy, growing ever larger in my body as I work. Incrementally, slowly, steadily, becoming slightly more invasive of the cells around it as each idea was transferred to the page. Transforming me in the very process of producing this book, stealthily turning me from the deepest interior of my being into a creature much closer to non-existence than the creature who began this writing. As I am writing this final contribution to the work, my life is drawing to a close, whether the end remains years distant or whether it will come—or if it has come already as you read this, which is not impossible—before this book even appears as a printed object to tell the tale.

I write this because I want magical thinking to work. I want my internal prayer to God to grant me more time, to put it off as long as it can be put off. Perhaps that prayer is not to be answered. Even so, having written this, I have still achieved what may be the only mastery over death that is possible.